T0339489

Cutting the Cost of Confusion

Confusion is more than just another daily inconvenience, though its impacts are often hidden in metrics such as market share, productivity, and ROI. This book shows how to identify and eliminate the Cost of Confusion in workplaces, marketplaces, and communities.

Cutting that cost demands the ability to distill, integrate, and synthesize ever more complex information from a broad range of perspectives and disciplines. Any gaps in understanding can and do negatively impact performance. Based on Richard Layton's 20 years of experience helping organizations to be heard and understood, this book offers a powerful universal lens to view the costly impacts of confusion and provides a framework to identify and manage the risk of failure to communicate with a range of stakeholders and audiences – and save millions of dollars in the process.

Decision-makers, practitioners, and students in marketing and advertising, organizational development, knowledge management, information technology, project management, and other fields will appreciate this unique set of insights and tools they can employ to great effect within their companies, organizations, and public institutions.

As Chief Clarity Officer of Transform Communications, **Rich Layton** works "under the hood" of global organizations to engage, educate, and inspire all those on whom success depends. Rich's "secret sauce" is a disciplined methodology that blends strategic communication with risk management, empowering leaders and teams to identify and overcome their organization's complex business, technology, and marketing challenges. The methodology and the mission are one and the same: *Cutting the Cost of Confusion.*

Cutting the Cost of Confusion

Eliminate the High Price of Failure to Communicate

Richard A. Layton

Routledge
Taylor & Francis Group

NEW YORK AND LONDON

Designed cover image: Getty

First published 2024
by Routledge
605 Third Avenue, New York, NY 10158

and by Routledge
4 Park Square, Milton Park, Abingdon, Oxon, OX14 4RN

Routledge is an imprint of the Taylor & Francis Group, an informa business

ISBN: 9781032293288 (hbk)
ISBN: 9781032293271 (pbk)
ISBN: 9781003301080 (ebk)

DOI: 10.4324/9781003301080

Typeset in Sabon
by Newgen Publishing UK

Graphics & Illustrations: Todd Farrell, times2studio

Contents

Preface

In the Information Age,
*THE GREATEST THREAT TO KNOWLEDGE
IS NOT IGNORANCE, BUT CONFUSION.*

It's not that we have too little information with which to make decisions as businesspeople, consumers, and voters; it's that we have far too much. From the boardroom to the store aisle to the voting booth, we stand paralyzed, deer awash in the high beams of facts, figures and competing claims for bigger profits, brighter whites, and better schools.

Decision paralysis is one of the myriad implications of Information Overload which have been researched for decades, first regarding mass marketing and advertising, and now in relation to the Internet and the emerging communications technologies it has spawned.

Compounding this data glut is the recognition that organizations and markets are complex and dynamic systems, like the planet itself. Understanding and managing these systems effectively demands the ability to distill, integrate and synthesize ever more information from a broad range of perspectives and disciplines. Thriving in the global economy demands that we do so masterfully—and faster than our competition.

Turning off the spigot is not an option. Facing the threat of confusion is imperative.

The inspiration for this book is the culmination of almost three decades experience helping organizations to be "heard and understood" among diverse groups on whom those organizations' success has depended, e.g., employees, investors, prospective customers, the general public, partners, voters, association members, etc. In case-after-case, I witnessed a direct relationship between the level of understanding/buy-in among these critical "success-holder" groups and performance metrics such as sales volume, market share, productivity, profit margin, return on investment, and other indicators of economic value.

During a series of high-level consulting assignments beginning in the mid-1990s, I began to recognize a recurring pattern associated with strategic change efforts such as corporate reorganizations, mergers and acquisitions, and major technology introductions. In virtually every instance, client organizations were experiencing substantial gaps between the value these high-level managed initiatives *promised* and what they *delivered*. In 1997, during a conversation with a colleague, a fitting term for these significant value gaps emerged: *The Cost of Confusion*.

Since that "personal epiphany", I have focused on developing a formal, disciplined methodology for helping organizations identify and minimize the Cost of Confusion wherever it presents itself. As that methodology has evolved and been embraced by my clients, several have realized, literally, millions of dollars of bottom-line benefits as a result. Even more gratifying is that the concept and approach have proved to be universal, applying as powerfully to branding, marketing, and advertising as to organizational development, knowledge management, information technology and beyond.

Therein lies my inspiration and best hope: That, as you read this book, you will come to experience a profound recognition of The Cost of Confusion and develop the ability to identify and eliminate it from your workplaces, marketplaces, and communities. To that end, following the chapters devoted to the pervasive nature of confusion and its impacts is a "how-to" methodology for "cutting the cost of confusion." It comes with no claims of being the last word on the subject; instead, it is a set of insights and tools offered as a starting point for anyone interested in creating more "meaning-full" companies, organizations, public institutions, and work lives.

Acknowledgements

During a phone conversation more than two decades ago, Mark Johnson, president of "The Understanding Business" (TUB), and I were trading "amens" about the many ways we had witnessed the consequences of poorly designed information in our clients' organizations. Mark spoke of a meeting with a major banking firm that had created and staffed a 15-person call center to handle questions about its employee benefits programs. Walking to the whiteboard, he led the executive management team in generating line-item estimates for salaries, office space, administrative/technical support, and other overhead associated with the department. Over a two-year period, the total had approached $1 million!

Putting down his felt-tip marker, Johnson needed both hands to pick up the company's Employee Benefits Manual. It was the classic three-ring binder filled with page after page of double-spaced double-speak. "This is the reason you need the benefits call center," he pronounced. "This manual is so dense, dry, and convoluted, that it does not enable employees to get the information or answers they need on their own. For $100,000, we can replace this manual with one that works, and you can have $900,000 back."

On the other end of the line, I let out a whistle and said, "Wow! It's like you helped them figure out their *cost of confusion*..."

For Mark Johnson and me, that was the first of many great idea exchanges related to bringing clarity and usefulness to complex information. I am forever grateful for his keen insights and observations. Another inspiration has been Mark's mentor, Saul Wurman, author of *Information Anxiety*. That book, given to me by a dear friend and creative partner (r.i.p., Cal Stanley), spent several years on the shelf; however, when I finally picked it up, Saul's ideas were a validation of much of the "shooting from the hip" that I had been doing for several years in my own communications consulting practice. It was a relief to discover that I hadn't been selling snake oil all those years!

A few other people come to mind for their unflagging support of my passion for organizational clarity: long-time client champions Jeff Heath of Marathon Petroleum, Greg Sills of Leading Projects, LLC, and Shawn Walker, Portfolio Materials Group, for trusting in my vision and allowing me to push the envelope; graphic design partners Amy and Todd Farrell (Times 2 Studio) and Phaedra Cook of Gecko Media for bringing all my napkin sketches to life; Greg Meenahan for the spiritual encouragement; attorney, author and dear friend, Susan Stoner, for her incisive editing; and to my wife Shelley for believing. She reminded me during discouraging times that my work "...isn't for the people who need it—it's for the people who want it."

Heartfelt thanks to Ken Lizotte of Emerson Consulting Group, who brought this literary Lazarus of a book back to life after it had languished for more than 20 years, and to the stalwart editorial team Meredith Norwich and her assistant Bethany Nelson at Routledge, Taylor & Francis Group.

Above all, thanks to the courageous clients who were willing to have their organizations and themselves *transformed*.

Rich Layton
January 2023

Chapter 1

Introduction

CONFUSION. To most people, it's a minor inconvenience, albeit an aggravating one, something most often associated with bad driving directions, ditzy salesclerks, and anything with the words "some assembly required" printed on the package.

But what if confusion was also something more insidious, something with potent economic implications for business, government, society—impacts often unrecognized or attributed mistakenly to other factors? Consider whether confusion might have played a hidden yet crucial role in:

- *The steady erosion of market share for a consumer powerhouse whose customers faced too many product choices among the company's leading brands*
- *Mission-critical information technology projects at Whirlpool, Nestle, and dozens of other major corporations which resulted in hundreds of millions of dollars in write-offs*
- *Mistrust of election integrity that began with Democrat Al Gore's closely fought battle for the Presidency on Election Day 2000 and now drives frightening levels of discord over election outcomes.*

These are just a few examples of the profound consequences when organizations and institutions fail to consider confusion and its potential effects on customers, employees, and the public.

What makes the challenge more daunting is that these cause-and-effect relationships are not something that auditors can find in the accounting system or that shareholders can see on the balance sheet; yet the bottom-line impacts are real. Here are a few of the myriad ways that confusion extracts its toll:

- **Lost sales** resulting from marketing and advertising that fail to win customers with clear and compelling reasons to purchase products and services

DOI: 10.4324/9781003301080-1

- **Lost productivity** resulting from organizational changes and technology initiatives which are not fully understood, accepted, and implemented by employees
- **Reduced shareholder value** resulting from mergers and acquisitions that fail to integrate cultures, processes, knowledge, and people for promised return-on-investment
- **Grid-locked public policy** resulting from overcomplicated debates which have alienated voters and enabled special interest groups to dominate

These and other critical implications of confusion are explored in specific examples in Chapters 2, 3, and 4. Each chapter focuses on a distinct organizational "audience"; i.e., customers, employees, and citizens. Through each chapter and unique example runs a common thread: the Cost of Confusion is real, and it has a demonstrated ability to drain value from the bottom line every minute of every day.

Confusion will never be eliminated, but it should always be anticipated and prepared to mitigate its negative impacts.

Confusion And Value Creation

To understand why confusion isn't just a modern inconvenience anymore, we need to ponder, for a moment, life in the Information Age and the Knowledge Economy to which it has given rise...

Today, value no longer derives primarily from natural resources and basic commodities but from millions of forms of intellectual capital, surfaced, recombined, and transmuted in countless ways by business organizations, market forces, and governing systems. The new raw materials of the Information Age and the Knowledge Economy are concepts and ideas for goods and services. Value is added by way of the technologies, processes, and procedures selected to bring those goods and services to market. Knowledge applied as innovation, enhancement, cost reduction or customization increases the value at each step in the life cycle. **Value creation** is now the core mission for relevant institutions of every kind, public or private, a mission that they accomplish by:

- leveraging information of every kind to create/add value across the enterprise
- fostering better, faster decision-making at every level of an organization
- maximizing business agility and speed-to-market
- becoming technology-enabled, not technology-encumbered

The concept of *survival of the fittest* has itself been subject to the forces of evolution, emerging as ***survival of the smartest***, i.e., those who can decipher the complex inter-connected nature of global commerce and can comprehend how to exploit their role in those systems by means of any and every potential competitive advantage.

From "Oil Bidness" To Knowledge Company

As an example of the tremendous economic reordering brought on by the Information Age, consider the transformation in the world of rough-necks and wildcatters. Just over a century ago, the famous Spindletop gusher near Beaumont, Texas, gave birth to the oil and gas industry and its focus on the discovery and exploitation of a finite natural resource. Against that Old Economy backdrop, what could such media "buzzwords" as *knowledge economy* and *knowledge workers* possibly have to do with finding and bringing oil out of the ground and into the marketplace? **EVERYTHING!**

In essence, *to exploit* a finite, naturally occurring resource means to get to it first, maximize its value for the lowest possible cost and sell it prof-itably in the marketplace. In each step of the process, success depends on being **smarter and faster than the competition**—smarter and faster at iden-tifying reserves, smarter and faster at drilling and production, smarter and faster at delivering to the wholesale and retail marketplace. Strategic tech-nology selection and continual innovation are other critical differentiators for performance.

Thus, while Exxon, BP, and others look like oil companies on the out-side, they are really **Knowledge Companies** on the inside. Fundamentally, their bottom-line performance is determined by **what they know**, the **processes and methods** they use to apply that knowledge, and how well they choose and use the **tools and technology** available to them. Knowledge—and an organization's ability to capture it, increase it, and apply it effectively—is what successful exploitation of oil and gas resources is all about.

Moreover, in the face of dwindling reserves, knowledge is the only means by which these companies can develop the alternative and renew-able energy resources which can ensure their futures. And it is at this time and place in their history that energy companies are beginning to grasp that people are their most valuable resource. Nevertheless, only some of these companies have begun to consider the impact of confusion on their day-to-day effectiveness.

Getting To "Yes": Why Confusion Is a Threat

With information and knowledge serving as the underlying currency of the 21st Century economy, the critical catalyst needed to "close the sale" is **understanding**. The exchange of value relies more than ever before on an intellectual foundation. Purchases, choices, votes, decisions, contract awards—all are the result of decision-making processes of one form or another, and all involve the processing of information.

Buying decisions, for instance, take place based on value propositions, marketing conversations, advertising campaigns, and detailed proposals that must be clearly understood by potential customers. To ensure satisfaction after the sale, that understanding must extend through instructions for use, customer service, and technical support. The entire value creation cycle exists within a context of rules, regulations and policies that govern marketplaces and the communities in which they operate.

Against this backdrop, the fundamental challenge is "getting to yes,"; whether it means closing the sale with a prospect, convincing employees to keep their focus on customer service, winning the support of a Wall Street analyst or educating a policymaker. Confusion poses a genuine threat at any point along this continuum.

For any organization to succeed in a landscape of such complexity demands an enormous capacity for critical thinking. It also requires a core capability to engage people and foster understanding across a wide range of audiences and stakeholder groups.

As illustrated in the accompanying chart, providing minimal engagement and no opportunity for genuine comprehension is how an organization

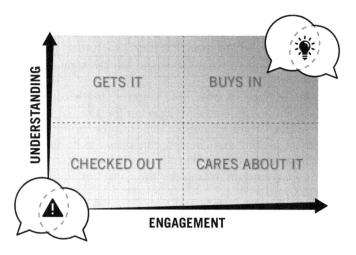

Figure 1.1

"gets to 'no' " with its constituents (lower left), i.e., no sale, no extra effort, no change, no vote, no solution.

Moving stakeholders along the vertical axis delivers minds, not hearts (upper left). Employees may learn a new business process, but unless they have a genuine connection to the organization, the new process will have minimal impact. In the case of customers, they may appreciate how the product works but have no interest in purchasing.

Moving stakeholders along the horizontal access deliver hearts, not minds (lower right). In the case of employees, there is plenty of enthusiasm, but performance falls short. In the case of consumers, these are people who purchase an item they care about but don't understand. It's a scenario that leads to high numbers of returns and overloads the product support team.

Effective organizations own the upper right corner. They are masters at eliminating confusion and securing the minds and hearts of employees, customers, and other stakeholder audiences. It's all about creating light bulb moments.

These are among the underlying dynamics of confusion that we will be exploring in real-world examples throughout this book.

The essential point to "understanding confusion" is that our knowledge-based society is a complex, multi-dimensional, and dynamic equation whose supreme common denominator is *people*. Human beings, and the various IQs (Intellectual Quotient) and EQs (Emotional Quotient) they represent, are inextricably woven into the way organizations, institutions, and socioeconomic systems operate. Confuse people—individually or collectively, at any point—as employees, buyers or voters, and the results can be costly, even catastrophic.

THIS IS THE WORLD IN WHICH CONFUSION STANDS AS A POWERFUL THREAT TO KNOWLEDGE AND ITS CAPACITY TO CREATE THRIVING BUSINESSES AND EFFICIENT INSTITUTIONS.

What Is the Cost of Confusion

If, as the saying goes, *Knowledge is Power*, then *Confusion is Paralysis*, carrying with it the potential to undermine productivity, encumber decision making and diminish return on investment for any organization that fails to identify and mitigate the risks. Confusion is bound, by its nature, by human nature, and by the workings of our economic system itself, to extract a price wherever it occurs. Quantify those effects, and you arrive at the **Cost of Confusion**® −

THE IMPACT (EXPRESSED IN DOLLARS) OF ADVERSE ECONOMIC EFFECTS RESULTING FROM LACK OF COMPREHENSION AMONG CUSTOMERS, EMPLOYEES, PARTNERS, AND OTHERS ON WHOM AN ORGANIZATION'S SUCCESS DEPENDS

Of course, this theme has several variations, depending on context. For example, in the realm of organizational change, the Cost of Confusion might be defined as "the difference between what a managed change effort promises and the financial results it actually delivers." A similar definition could be applied to mergers and acquisitions or to an information technology project. Chances are an appropriate definition of the Cost of Confusion can be developed for any situation involving *complexity* and *people*.

Calculating the associated costs is more of a common-sense approach than a mathematical formula. It starts with the question, "How might a lack of understanding have an impact in this situation?" The example mentioned in the *Acknowledgements* section bears repeating. A nationwide bank was so overwhelmed by employees' questions about benefits and insurance that the company created a 15-person call center to provide information. Through estimating average salaries, calculating square footage for the department's offices, and adding costs for furniture, computers and administrative support, the senior management team realized the bank had incurred almost $1 million in unbudgeted expenses over two years to address problems that stemmed from an inadequate benefits communication package. That amount represented their Cost of Confusion. Six months after investing $100,000 to revamp the package, the bank shut down the call center <u>and</u> returned $900,000 to the bottom line.

(Note to concerned readers—throughout subsequent chapters, there will be plenty of opportunities to practice calculating the Cost of Confusion.)

Confusion Is Risky Business

Still skeptical whether something as seemingly abstract as confusion has an identifiable, quantifiable cost? Don't forget the infamous "butterfly ballot" that many experts argue cost Al Gore the presidency. Confusion over which punch card hole corresponded to which candidate resulting in thousands of discarded ballots, "hanging chad" notwithstanding. Despite the historic impact, this example might be confusing in its simplest form. The confusion giving rise to that incident stemmed from the way in which the information was physically presented, e.g., how it was worded and laid out on a page, form, or other document; what was included, what was left out.

At the other end of the spectrum is confusion associated with complexity at an intellectual level, e.g., a hard-to-grasp concept, technical explanation, or value proposition. Take, for example, any of the hundreds of "dot-bombs", companies whose failure to create and sustain value often stemmed from the inability to communicate said value to customers, investors, analysts, trading partners, and many other audiences on whom any real success would depend. Emerging technologies, public policy debates, complicated election initiatives... the greater the intellectual complexity, the greater the potential threat from confusion.

Un-Confusion: The Zen of Organizational Effectiveness

Taking a cue from the *Un-Cola advertising* campaign for lemon-lime soft drink **7-Up®**, one way to grasp the Cost of Confusion concept is to consider its opposite; in this case, an organizational state of being that is as free from confusion and its negative impacts as is humanly possible.

Researchers have long studied so-called "Zen moments" of peak performance that athletes, artists, musicians and other creative professionals speak of in reverent, mystical tones. *The Flow, the Zone, the Groove...* there are many names for the concept, but the experience itself is universal. In a heartbeat, years of studying, training, and practice converge in precise alignment. Time seems to stand still as all barriers, physical and mental, fall away. Every synapse fires precisely at the ideal instant. Every muscle cell delivers its packet of energy at just the right nanosecond. Every movement is perfect in its economy. Every instinct is on target. It is a moment of true effortlessness.

If biology can galvanize millions of individual cells in a synchronous level of peak performance, why can't an organization aspire to that same state? Why not a Zen of organizational effectiveness? Why not strive for a deliberate mastery of purpose that is the antithesis of confusion?

Imagine a clarity of thought and action expressed in thousands of moment-to-moment choices in which employees opt for doing the best right thing in any given situation: genuinely solving a customer problem, patiently defusing a manager's objection to a new idea, clocking in each day with a life's worth of knowledge and experience, not just meeting the requirements in the job description.

The goal is to achieve as many of these moments as possible, instances in which the behavior of each member of the enterprise combines to express that organization is operating as its perfect self. Through knowledge and understanding delivered as a core capability, every individual is connected clearly to his or her purpose in the organization. That is the ultimate promise of work in the Information Age.

For an organization, it means "getting to 'yes'" on a hundred fronts, hundreds of thousands of times a day, not only with employees but also with customers, investors, suppliers... all the stakeholders on whom that organization's success depends. That is the ultimate promise of the Cost of Confusion reduced to zero!

From Concept to Reality

Subsequent chapters of this book highlight examples of the Cost of Confusion and its quantifiable impacts on employees, customers, citizens, and nations. For those readers ready to take on the challenge of Cutting the Cost themselves, the concluding chapter presents a set of best practice communications tools and an integrated methodology to help organizations uncover, address and mitigate the risks that confusion presents.

If there is a compelling central theme to take away from this book, it is this:

> *Confusion in all its forms—from minor inconvenience to information overload and decision paralysis—must be viewed as a potential risk to the success and effectiveness of every business organization, government agency, or public institution.*
>
> *Failure to do so is to accept a permanent and ever-widening gap between that which we aspire to and that which we achieve.*

QUICKSTART: A GUIDE TO KEY CONCEPTS AND TERMINOLOGY

A brief description of various emotional, psychological, and behavioral elements helpful to understanding the causes, consequences, and countermeasures involving the Cost of Confusion.

Benefits Realization

Taking a 360-degree view of a strategic initiative to surface and address critical indirect factors that may inhibit the effort from achieving all its desired business impact *(Examples: conflicting goals and incentives across departments, misalignment of workflow, gaps in skills and competencies, etc.)*

Complicated versus Complex

Core differentiators of information, these terms often are used interchangeably. *Complicated* applies to processes, mechanisms and products that are comprised of a significant number of components assembled through a fixed sequence of steps to completion. *Complex* applies to endeavors that involve significant variables, dynamic decision making, and adaptation to changing conditions. Examples: Geometry is complicated. Calculus is complex. Mutual funds are complicated. Financial derivatives are complex. In terms of communication, a complicated process can be simplified to a large extent, but a complex process has a lower limit past which it cannot be distilled accurately or meaningfully.

Decision-driven Marketing

A methodology that aligns marketing communication content and touch points with the "customer journey," i.e., the process by which prospects seek out information, digest it and arrive at their decision to purchase. This approach sets out to "educate the customer" in such a proactive way that those competitors are rarely considered, and the desired buying decision is a forgone conclusion.

Decision Mapping

A business intelligence methodology for analyzing decisions based on their potential impacts on stakeholders; surfaces "hot button issues" for decision makers and informs strategies for framing critical decisions and influencing outcomes.

Decision Paralysis

Term for the tendency that human beings have to shut down when the number and/or complexity of choices exceeds the capacity to analyze, compare and contrast key factors, resulting in no decision at all (aka Analysis Paralysis).

Information Overload

It's well documented that life in the modern world includes a constant bombardment of information in a non-stop battle for each person's attention. The same onslaught takes place daily inside organizations in every corner of the globe, leaving individuals struggling to know what to pay attention to and how to make sense of it. Countering this overload requires controlling the amount of information an audience is subject to and ensuring all information is meaningful, practical, and applicable.

Information Underwhelm

First impressions determine whether a target audience member stops and devotes time and attention to critical content. Generic, underwhelming information might educate, but it cannot inspire, thus surrendering a significant amount of its potential to educate, motivate, and impact. The competition for attention and "mindshare" has elevated the art of presentation. It is now essential to package content in ways that engage audiences that are used to a steady diet of sophisticated online video, graphics, and animation.

Information Quality

Confusion generally is associated with a lack of understanding, but it also can result from "bad" information. There is a range of attributes involved in information quality, including accuracy, completeness, consistency, uniqueness, timeliness, relevance, and more. Deficiencies in any of these attributes can introduce risk into decision-making, workflows, sales, and other critical performance areas.

Information Taxonomy

A coherent hierarchical structure developed to organize a complex body of expert knowledge for user access, application, and phased learning. Typically serves as a basis for website development and internal portals (e.g., SharePoint).

Rate of Information Transfer

The speed and efficiency with which various media deliver essential information to workers and potential customers. *(Especially important in a world of decreasing attention spans.)*

ROE: Return on Effort

A simple ratio between the value delivered and the time/activity/aggravation expended.

Speed-to-Know

Communications and training that focus strategically on expediency, immediate practical application and "just-in-time" delivery to ensure workforce proficiency.

Value-driven Knowledge Management

An approach to organizing and delivering information in order to optimize value creation, i.e., getting the right information to the right people at precisely the right time they need it to maximize their workflow contributions.

Chapter 2

The Cost of Confusing Customers

The impact of confusion inside an organization can go undetected for years so long as there is sufficient revue to offset the cost. But it's a different story when it comes to customers. Decreasing sales, declining market share, costly returns, and eroding brand reputation are a few of the metrics signaling customers are confused. Perhaps, they don't understand the benefits and features or don't appreciate how much more value a new product offers over its established competitors. For start-up ventures, particularly those in technology, the cost of confusion could even mean failure to launch.

This chapter highlights a range of examples from three business sectors in which the cost of confusion is an ever-present business risk:

CONSUMER RETAIL | TECHNOLOGY | HEALTHCARE

Retail Confusion: Understanding how people reach a buying decision

Early on in my research, I spent time in a variety of stores observing people as they shopped for products stocked typically on crowded shelves and hanging displays. Two of the most intriguing aisles were among the personal products section: toothpaste and razors. Within these two categories alone, manufacturers have provided a dizzying array of choices. It was rare to see a shopper make a "grab-and-go" selection on either aisle. For toothpaste, most shoppers spent several minutes picking up item after item, reading their labels, and placing them back on the shelf. This process was repeated five or six times until one lucky winner went into the shopping cart. Sometimes, that winner would be the store brand. Overwhelmed by options, shoppers reached for the toothpaste that came in one flavor and size.

The activity was similar for razors. Shoppers lingered here even longer, jockeying for position to reach out and take packages off the hanging displays. What brand of razor, which type of handle, and how many blades in

DOI: 10.4324/9781003301080-2

the cartridge? In this aisle, compatibility is of the essence, but it is complicated and time-consuming to determine. Occasionally, I watched someone walk away from the razor refills display without making any selection at all. Perhaps it was exasperation or fear of bringing home the wrong thing. Whatever the case, the store lost a sale.

Too Much of a Good Thing

Fortunately, we are on the backside of the era of "peak product" that took place in the years leading up to the 2008 Recession. During peak product, Proctor & Gamble sold 72 formulas under its Pantene hair care brand. Kleenex tissue came in nine varieties. Kellogg's stopped moms in their tracks at the freezer case to choose from 16 flavors of Eggo Waffles.

As the number of products proliferated, the average length of a weekly shopping trip increased. More products meant more decisions and more time to scan all the options. At the extreme end of effects, some shoppers experience **decision paralysis.** They get stuck, unable to make a purchase because they feel overwhelmed by the sheer number of varieties or the need to study information on every label. Some shoppers fear they will make the "wrong" choice by failing to bring home a "less-than-the-best" version of the product for themselves or their families.

We've all been there—afraid that our family won't have the whitest sheets or that we'll be scolded for bringing home the wrong flavor of their favorite cookies, cereal, or mouthwash.

In addition to decision paralysis among shoppers, the proliferation of confusing product lines created the opportunity for major retailers to develop the **store brand.** The store brand strategy focused on attracting shoppers through lower costs and pared-down lineups of "knock-off" products. Store brands aim for negligible differences in quality from the traditional product and provide significantly better margins for the retailer.

Fortunately, the world is on the other side of "peak product," with leading consumer brands scaling back and eliminating subcategories sold under such original banners as Colgate®, Crest®, Dove®, Tide®, Dawn® and thousands of other household names. Meanwhile, the battle for shelf space continues to intensify as retail store brands become serious challengers to the world's leading consumer products manufacturers.

Response Strategies

Streamlining the brand, slimming down the portfolio, rationalizing the product mix... whatever the term, it's an exercise every manufacturer and service provider can benefit from. Look first at the revenue mix within the primary product category. Typically, a core group of items will account for the bulk of sales. The outliers are the obvious places to reexamine and revalidate the business case for maintaining each of them. Be aware that some items may have die-hard fans. When a company eliminates items with which shoppers have a long history and a bit of sentimental attachment, there is a risk of public relations fallout on social media platforms.

For a deeper dive, take the time to survey key customers about why they choose certain varieties regularly over others. This information can be used to validate marketing strategies, align features/benefits, and ensure that customers are buying the products for the reasons you think they are. It also warrants looking at how competitors' product lines are organized and positioned in the market. Are they leveraging the simplicity of chocolate and vanilla or the variety of 31 flavors?

Clarify and Close—or Confuse and Lose

Every "touch point" with a potential customer provides an opportunity to present a compelling value proposition. While features and benefits are vital to converting prospects into purchasers, the packaging, timing, and delivery of key information impact marketplace success as surely as the products and services themselves. Increasingly, the marketing mindset has undergone a radical shift from making the sale to educating the prospect. The latter is driven by helping potential customers arrive at a buying decision they can feel good about without feeling unduly pressured. One outgrowth of this shift is content marketing.

The concept involves developing information that pertains to a company's products and services and then sharing it online through a wide range of digital channels, including social media. Content may be packaged as videos, blogs, posts, and digital downloads. The overarching objective is to establish the company as a trusted source of valid and valuable insights for prospects and customers. This approach typically relies on brevity and a narrow topic focus that reduces the risk of confusion during the early stages of relationship building with potential customers.

> We created too many variations on our Bowflex home gyms, and it ended up confusing consumers. What happens when they have too many choices? They don't make any decisions. Ron Arp, Nautilus, Inc. (The Oregonian, 1/6/08)[1]

"Decision-driven Marketing" is a variation of the concept, aligning the scope and cadence of content with the process that large organizations use to identify, select and purchase big-ticket items.

The inspiration was a client's struggle to introduce laser barcode technology into the paper-driven world of warehouse distribution. Prospects need to be shepherded along a steep learning curve to understand the "revolutionary" impact of the technology. The marketing system was designed to parallel the buyer's journey with informational materials specific to the customer's research, due diligence, review, and selection activities. While competitors emphasized their technologies, my client provided white papers, information graphics, and other media intended to educate the direct users, internal referrers, economic decision makers, and all other stakeholders. Potential customers made use of my client's marketing materials at each stage of the selection process. As a result, my client's technology solution had the highest visibility and the most credibility going into the final phase of vendor selection. The outstanding close rate confirmed the effectiveness of the approach. It has since become embedded in the company's sales and marketing functions.

There are several other strategies that center on enabling customers to make well-informed purchases from among complicated product lines and complex technologies. The approaches can range from product guides and comparison charts that shoppers can refer to in the store aisle to websites containing product recommendation scripts. The latter allows prospects to "self-qualify" through a series of questions and choices that funnels potential customers to the most appropriate product/solution for their business needs.

There are several other strategies that center on enabling customers to make well-informed purchases from among complicated product lines and complex technologies. Product guides and comparison charts offer immediate assistance to shoppers in the store aisle. Online options include product comparisons, recommendations, and reviews. Some websites include product recommendation functions that take visitors through a series of yes/no questions and multiple-choice options. Based on the selected answers, prospects are funneled through the full range of available offerings to land on the most appropriate product/solution for their business needs.

Snapshot: They Glazed Over Like a Christmas Ham

As the benefits program consultants tried to explain stop loss coverage and utilization rates, I watched the eyes in the audience of blue-collar union leaders glaze over like a proverbial Christmas ham. The benefits sales team had no clue that the biggest sale in their firm's history had just slipped away. It was a lost opportunity, too, as this was a game-changing benefits option that would have been a win/win/win for the workers' union, its public agency employer, and the taxpayers who funded the mass transit system.

My client, the union's attorney, was counting on the consulting firm to help bring everybody on board. Unfortunately, the consultants failed to recognize the need for critical adjustments in their standard terminology and narrative. During the discussion of "stop loss," for example, I wanted to jump in and say, "You know, like overdraft protection on your checking account." There was no attempt to connect unfamiliar concepts with things the audience routinely grasped. In the end, it was a triumph of the **Cost of Confusion:** No sale – with a nice slice of ham on the side.

CONFUSING TECHNOLOGY

Admittedly, this is the low-hanging fruit in every discussion of complexity and confusion, particularly when consumer electronics are involved. It is the nature of innovation to create products that are *ahead of the curve* when introduced to their intended market. The capacity of potential buyers to grasp the benefits of new technologies and choose to purchase them is not universal. Consequently, manufacturers rely on "early adopters" to champion lifestyle innovations, generate buzz, and jumpstart market momentum.

The size of the gap between sales to Early Adopters and the tipping point at which a technology ramps toward mainstream acceptance can be quantified as a Cost of Confusion.. Closing that gap may take years and requires companies to have sufficient reserves to underwrite product lines until a technology "catches on" with the public. There is also the underlying risk that a product never achieves sufficient traction in the marketplace and a sales inflection point never arrives.

One of my most compelling object lessons regarding this principle came from a visit to my local Best Buy in early 2015. My son and I discovered that the store had replaced its music department with a new Connected Home section. This was in response to the first wave of products from the Internet of Things—devices that would control thermostats, set lighting for every mood, stream a soundtrack for any occasion, lower our shades, and lock our doors at night.

There was little to no professional merchandising in evidence, just boxes of random devices lined up on the top shelf. In subsequent store visits over the course of the next few years, I rarely saw any shoppers in that aisle, even during the peak holiday shopping season.

Eventually, sales did pick up as more homeowners began to appreciate the benefits of programmable thermostats and were introduced to "Alexa," Amazon's ubiquitous personalized digital assistant. Video doorbells have continued the trend.

Subsequently, Best Buy's Connected Home section has grown and now incorporates a significant amount of point-of-purchase information to help educate customers about features and connectivity. Yet the reality is that sales remain constrained by the fog of confusion that permeates the market more than a decade after its vaunted launch.

Overpromise, underdeliver

The original premise of the fully connected home is undermined by the inherent complexity of the various devices needed to achieve it. Individual setup of devices is time-consuming and frustrating for all but the most tech-savvy homeowners. Integrating a range of products to create a truly smart home is more daunting due to conflicting standards/protocols for wireless communications and connectivity. Determining which devices are compatible is not for the technically faint-of-heart and likely has constrained sales to consumers with no appetite for the steep IT learning curve required to install and use these technologies to their fullest potential.

"Too many people got burned," declared Lewis Hosier of Wired World Technologies. "Cost is no object for our clients, so many of them insisted on including smart home devices when designing their new homes and undertaking major remodels. What those owners didn't realize is that they were at the 'bleeding edge' of this technology. It was extremely complicated to integrate, labor-intensive to program and less than intuitive to operate. For the most part, our clients were disillusioned and disappointed by their smart home investment." [2]

For Hosier, there was a sense that manufacturers just threw smart home devices into the marketplace and waited to see what would stick. The early adopters among Wired World Technologies' clients had the potential to be strong positive influencers with their high net-worth peers; instead, they likely prevented sales by sharing their technology frustrations across their social circles and professional networks.

Despite the plethora of Amazon Echo and Google Dot "digital assistants" on countertops around the world, the promise of the smart home remains unfulfilled, as evidenced by sales figures that have lagged the industry's optimistic growth projections year after year. What's more, the smart-home market landscape has quite a few skeletons of startups that were unable to survive the slow rate of adoption for their devices.

Antenna to Internet

Lagging adoption rate is a pattern that has been repeated throughout the consumer electronics marketplace, particularly when a new technology requires a fundamental rethinking of what came before it. The transition from black and white to color was an evolutionary upgrade for the broadcast television industry. The first serious disruption emerged around 1977 with the arrival of video cassette recorders. VCRs (and blank cassettes) introduced the world to *time-shifting,* the ability to watch a show any time after its initial broadcast over the air.

Twenty years later, the venerable VCR was challenged – partially – when the Digital Video Disc arrived to supplant bulky pre-recorded VHS tapes. The shift was partial because it applied only to prerecorded content, not to broadcast TV. The DVD expanded upon the technology of shiny plastic compact discs with players that offered consumers convenient home viewing of theatrical movies and previously released TV shows. However, the DVD did not upend how people accessed their traditional network and cable programming.

That would arrive just two years later, in 1997 with the introduction of the PVR – Personal Video Recorder. The technology caused a tectonic shift in what it means to watch television. Essentially, the PVR was a digital version of the VCR. The new devices were purpose-built minicomputers that recorded programming onto their hard drives. Overnight, the bulky mechanical technology and inconvenience of analog VCRs became obsolete.

Two manufacturers, TiVo and ReplayTV, took the concept of time-shifting to the next level and beyond. In the process, their technology upended the industry by pushing analog broadcast stations and antennas aside in favor of digital transmission. These devices required an Internet connection and a monthly subscription, adding to the cost of confusion for manufacturers– and the cost of ownership for potential customers.

"I don't believe I truly understood what Tivo did, what it was for, or why I'd appreciate it." Joshua Rafofsky, technology consultant. (WSJ,2/7/2001)[3]

After experiencing a failure to take off, PVR makers recognized the obstacles and did make efforts to educate retailers and consumers by way of traveling roadshows, in-store demos, and multi-million-dollar ad campaigns. Tivo, for example, sent a 40-foot demo truck around the U.S. to Nascar races and other public gatherings to demonstrate how its PVR works.

Still, as sales continued to lag expectations, stock prices plunged. Ultimately, the first movers of the personal TV revolution lost the long game to satellite and cable companies offering their own Digital Video Recorders to subscribers. ReplayTV sold its assets in 2007, and TiVo remains a niche player. Tivo's "failure to launch" story remains a cautionary tale for consumer electronics manufacturers.

Although the first movers did not maintain their market advantage, their technology changed the landscape. Consumers today take for granted the ability to search for their favorite shows and set-up "season passes" to record every episode. Freed from the network schedules, viewers are empowered to watch what they went when they want, using the remote to skip commercials, pause to make popcorn, or replay a subtle plot twist.

Like the VCR before it, the DVR is being eclipsed by the remarkable ascent of video streaming. Viewers can watch whatever they want, wherever they want, and whenever they want. With its subscription-based digital streaming platform, Netflix leveraged first-mover advantage to become the dominant player worldwide. The advantage has been steadily chipped away as dozens of other big players have entered the market to compete for monthly subscribers. Hollywood studios, major broadcast networks, global publishing giants, and even Apple are among the heavyweights currently slugging it out for dominance. Industry experts predict a big shakeout is imminent as consumers experience subscription overload and start culling the number of services they pay for monthly.

Confusion After the Sale

Although sales figures are significant indicators of the Cost of Confusion, there is another metric to consider: customer returns. The issue came to the forefront after research by Accenture (WSJ, 5/8/08)[4] estimated that the consumer electronics industry spent $13.8 billion to handle returns of newly purchased items. The return rates varied between 11% and 20% among such categories as wireless phone systems, home networking gear, and smart TVs. Only 5% of the returns were defective products; the majority fell under the category of "didn't meet expectations." The study found that many consumers simply gave up because their new purchases were too confusing to operate and enjoy. Retail experts estimate that the cost to process, inspect, repackage, restock, and resell returned items ranges from 15% to 30% of the original purchase price.

The consequences don't stop there. Of those who do return an item, almost 25% avoid that same brand from then on. In other words, brands with high return rates can lose those customers for life. Retailers can take a hit as well when some of those customers unhappy with the brand show their displeasure by never shopping at the same retailer again.

In response, manufacturers have begun to expand their focus to both before and after the purchase. Planning for long-term customer satisfaction starts by helping potential buyers to choose the model that is the best fit for their budget, lifestyle, and level of technical sophistication. Buyer guides, comparison charts, explicit information about additional services needed (e.g., high-speed Internet), and accessories (e.g., HDMI cable) reduce the customer's risk of disappointment or the shock of realizing more spending is needed before the new device can be enjoyed.

Focusing on after the sale turns out to be even more important. According to Copilot, a post-purchase customer experience platform, 65% of consumer electronics returns are the result of issues during setup *(source: PYMTS.com)[5]*. Manufacturers realize the importance of providing accessible, easy-to-understand guidance on how to set up and operate new devices. Initially, this information was provided via step-by-step user guides featuring helpful graphics and troubleshooting tips.

Today, the return process has changed. Now, new owners initiate product setup and orientation by using their smart phone to scan a QR Code on the side of the box. The process unfolds online through a scripted series of dialog boxes and confirmations as each step in the sequence is completed. Hours of trial-and-error frustration are condensed to ten minutes or less, at the conclusion of which people are left with more time to watch favorite shows, surf the Internet, or enjoy their go-to podcasts.

Another strategy by manufacturers is offering "concierge service" for big-ticket items such as large-screen smart TVs and high-resolution video projectors. Because these products are complex and have a prohibitively high cost of return, many major retailers and manufacturers have invested in offering turnkey delivery and in-home set-up services, typically for a nominal fee. The presence of knowledgeable technicians onsite helps to minimize customer frustration and prevents problems due to "operator error." Ensuring the correct setup and walking customers through the basics of using their new devices is the best insurance there is against costly returns of aggressively priced electronics.

Putting User Experience at the Core

As I noted at the start of this section, technology is low hanging fruit when discussing the Cost of Confusion. No doubt, everyone reading this book has had dozens of frustrating personal experiences over years of wrestling with new technology at work and home. For those who are part of an enterprise seeking success through innovative applications and breakthrough technology, the first commandment is "Thou Shalt Not Confuse." The more complex the offering, the more challenging it is to keep that commandment.

No company has taken this commandment more seriously than Apple. From the outset, the company focused on creating an alternative user experience to the PC. The design of its products and their intuitive operating systems set Apple apart from all others and gave rise to the world's most ubiquitous technology ecosystem.

Apple recognized the critical importance of turning customers into fans by helping them become highly proficient at using the company's hardware and software. The introduction of **the Genius Bar** in 2001 signaled a first-of-its-kind commitment to building and sustaining a lifelong relationship with everyone who purchased an Apple product. The Genius Bar offered customers the ability to schedule an in-store appointment to meet one-on-one with a product expert for help. It was a radical notion and required a substantial ongoing investment in infrastructure and talent. The concept has since grown to include a massive online knowledge base and a variety of user communities. Apple's hands-on, personalized tech support continues to be a powerful mechanism for instilling brand loyalty and driving repeat business across Apple's premium-priced product lines.

Laptop on Wheels

The newest target-rich environment for technology confusion is the accelerating global conversion to electric vehicles. It's a seismic shift not only in the powerplant of the automobile but also in the nature of the driving experience. The traditional instrument dashboard has been replaced by a touchscreen interface that redefines how drivers control their "transportation devices."

In its rapid rise to market domination, EV manufacturer Tesla has taken whole chapters from the Apple playbook. Engineers designed the cars around an intuitive driver interface that is a central theme of the company's marketing and sales. At Tesla stores, the showroom interaction focuses on how to use the touchscreen system, and representatives provide additional orientation for those taking cars out to test drive. (Author's disclosure: my wife took delivery of a Tesla Model Y during the writing of this book.)

Like Apple, Tesla has its equivalent Genius Bar for new owners and reaches out to them after their first month of ownership to schedule a one-on-one session. The purpose is to answer any questions owners may

---

THE SELF-CHECKOUT LINE

Please insert your own frustrating personal anecdote here. Thank You!
      – The Author

have after driving their cars for several months. This interaction also continues customer education by introducing new features added as part of Tesla's ongoing software upgrades. For the first time in automotive history, purchasing a new car means signing up for a lifelong technology learning curve.

Thus far, no other EV manufacturer has closed the gap on Tesla's vehicle interface. Reviews of competitors' cars routinely point to the shortcomings of their software and less-than-intuitive operation. In all fairness, the established global brands have decades of "inside-the-box" thinking to overcome. Tesla did not, and its ability to transform the relationship between cars and their drivers is one of the reasons owners are so fiercely loyal to their Teslas, despite the quality control problems the company battled early on. Interesting to note that people are not returning their new Teslas because their owners find them too confusing!

Takeaways for Technology Sellers

The promise of every new technology is that it will make our lives better, easier, faster, cheaper, and more enjoyable. Rarely does that list include "simpler." Adding new technology to our lives almost always involves a learning curve that begins before the sale and continues well after. Manufacturers and retailers that fail to own that curve and help people navigate it leave themselves wide open to the cost of confusion. That may not matter to a technology company that just wants to make a sale, but it's not a sustainable business model. Confusion can prevent sales, generate costly

Smart Phones / Dumb Owners

We used to be smart people with dumb phones—now, it's just the opposite! According to recent industry estimates, 85% of Americans own a smartphone. Yet, tens of millions of users can barely keep up with the explosion of features their devices offer. Across all age groups, smartphones remain confounding and intimidating, essentially being reduced to expensive cameras that can make calls. The disconnect between mobile phone capabilities and the capacity of people to take advantage of them represents a staggering Cost of Confusion. What's the point of technology products so sophisticated that they make their owners feel inadequate and overwhelmed? What strategies do you and/ or your organization use to put users' capabilities ahead of features and their complexity?

returns, and permanently drive away potential customers. Manufacturers of consumer electronics or other home and office technology products must think in terms of educating their potential customers and then supporting them after the sale so they can derive the full value of ownership.

Healthcare Confusion

Beginning with doctors' penchant for illegible handwriting, the field of medicine and healthcare has engendered more confusion than any other aspect of modern living. This is a realm in which failure to communicate can have life-and-death consequences. On a more mundane level, confusion drives inconvenience, inefficiency, and ineffectiveness throughout the healthcare system.

A fundamental challenge is the difficulty people naturally have processing information when they are emotionally overwhelmed. Fear, uncertainty, concern, dread, and other negative emotions release stress hormones that can trigger fight-or-flight responses that impair cognitive ability. Consequently, hospitals, doctors' offices, and other medical facilities are prime environments for fostering confusion. At the same time, providers dealing with fast-paced, high stress working conditions are at higher risk of making errors in diagnosis, treatment, surgery, and medication.

All the above takes place within the convoluted ecosystem of private health insurance, government programs, and healthcare bureaucracy, resulting in an exponential increase in the number of opportunities for confusion.

The Doctor Will Confuse You Now

Historically, the doctor's office has been the frontline in the patient's battle to understand and benefit from quality medical care. In most cases, an educational and cultural gap of eight to twelve years separates doctors from their patients and their patience. Even the most educated Americans struggle with "health literacy," defined as the ability to hear, read, comprehend, and act on verbal and written information coming from medical professionals. Moreover, after leaving the office, most patients forget much of what the doctors have told them. Moreover, what they do remember is often inaccurate. For patients from lower educational and socioeconomic levels or with different cultural backgrounds, the health literacy gap can be enormous.

"We are dealing with complicated medical issues and expecting patients to take more and more responsibility for their own care," says David W. Baker, chief of the division of internal medicine at Northwestern

Memorial Hospital in Chicago and a leading researcher in doctor-patient communication. "But what we are asking of patients is frequently beyond their capacity to comprehend this information." (WSJ, 7/3/2003)[6] (The consequences of this failure to comprehend are profound. Patients who are unable to fully process and understand their diagnosis can fail to comply with prescribed treatment, make mistakes with medication and abandon follow-up care. The impact is especially acute regarding chronic illness. When conditions such as hypertension and asthma are left untreated or undertreated, the health consequences can be dire for the patient and result in tens of billions of dollars a year in avoidable costs to healthcare systems and social programs.

In response to this recognized problem, promoting health literacy has become a major policy-level initiative in recent years, spanning community, state, and national efforts. Fostering greater awareness of health literacy best practices has had benefits for consumers and medical professionals alike. Increasingly, patients are taking notes during their doctors' appointments and bringing family members along to ask questions and ensure vital information does not get lost in translation or forgotten. Doctors, in turn, are encouraged to drop complex medical jargon in place of plain-spoken layman's terminology; for example, referring to the risk of "heart attack" instead of "myocardial infarction."

No word yet, however, on whether doctors are signing up for remedial penmanship classes.

Confusion Gets Hospitalized

When treatment escalates beyond the relative comfort of their doctor's office, patients face a daunting new environment, one that has exponentially more opportunities for confusion. Hospitals and specialized medical centers rely on increased technology, large scale, and higher patient volume to achieve their goals. That complexity makes it even more difficult to communicate clearly with patients. It also has the potential to confuse members of the healthcare staff as well.

Of course, being handed a felt tip marker and told to draw a big "X" on the knee that's not being replaced doesn't exactly inspire a patient's confidence. Nonetheless, simple procedures like this have been widely adopted to help ensure absolute clarity when going into surgery. Taking a cue from pilots, surgeons, and operating room personnel have begun to embrace pre-flight "checklists" of instruments, tools and supplies to prevent complications during and after surgery and stem the rise of malpractice claims.

Managing patient expectations for surgery is another target-rich area for clarity. Realistic patient expectations improve surgical outcomes and reduces the exposure of doctors and hospitals to malpractice claims.

Information graphics, illustrations, and video animation are being used to educate patients prior to routine procedures such as knee and hip replacements, colonoscopies, cardiac stents, and more.

The intent of this enhanced communication is to have patients see the step-by-step procedures they are signing up for and develop a clear picture of their responsibilities during each stage of their recovery. Typically, patients receive email links to view specific education programs at their convenience – and well ahead of upcoming surgeries – providing ample time to ask questions and address concerns in advance. Frequently, these informative systems also create an electronic audit trail to use as a defense if patients falsely claim they were not made aware of all possible risks and complications.

When Details Fall Through the Cracks

Confusion isn't just about a lack of understanding. It also can be caused by a lack of high-quality information passing among medical professionals. This reflects the fact that the value of information is not fixed; rather, it depends on a combination of essential attributes including accuracy, completeness, consistency, uniqueness, timeliness, relevance, and more. Information value plummets when the intended recipient gets too little, incorrect, or out-of-date information. Low value information has been a significant contributing factor in medical errors that seriously compromise in-hospital care. An example might be a patient receiving a second dose of a previously administered drug or a doctor using a defibrillator on a patient who has a Do Not Resuscitate directive in place.

It is well-known that patient safety is at its most vulnerable during shift changes when the status of each patient must be accurately conveyed to the incoming staff assuming responsibility for a patient floor or specialty care unit. Vital patient information that falls through the cracks during these hand-offs can result in medication errors, erroneous treatment protocols, and failure to note indicators of worsening health.

While all hospitals recognize the need for consistent hand-off of patients, informal procedures have long been the norm. The non-profit Institute for Healthcare Improvement has made this issue a key focus of its research and development. To address potential communication breakdowns, the group introduced a communication model known as **SBAR—Situation, Background, Assessment, and Recommendation.** SBAR was adapted by Kaiser Permanente from the procedures used during the change of command on nuclear submarines! (WSJ, 6/28/2006)[7]

The following is an example of how nurses and physicians follow the **SBAR framework** to communicate concisely and completely when handing off patients during a shift change.

Situation: Describe the patient

- Identify self, unit, patient, room number
- Briefly state the condition/diagnosis, when it happened or started, and how severe

Background: Provide pertinent background information, e.g.:

- The admitting diagnosis and date of admission
- List of current medications, allergies, IV fluids, and labs
- Most recent vital signs
- Lab results: provide the date and time any tests were done and results of previous tests for comparison
- Other clinical information

Assessment: Summarize the condition of the patient and any changes noted during the prior shift.

- Overall condition of the patient, including symptoms
- Any treatment administered and patient's response
- Code status

Patient-friendly Admission Process

For years, patients coming through the door for major surgery in a renowned regional medical center were handed a thick welcome package at the front desk and shown to their rooms. Typically feeling overwhelmed and nervous, the new arrivals then had a string of hospital administrators knocking at the door, presenting more paperwork and forms to be signed. With so much activity, most patients never had a chance to "get their bearings" in advance of their surgeries, learn what would be involved in recovery, or know what to do when it was time to check out. Consequently, nurses bore the brunt of patient questions over and over during their shifts... *When can my family visit me? Where is the cafeteria? What happens when I am discharged?*

To remove that distraction and provide consistent information to incoming patients, our team proposed a single-point delivery solution using the in-house TV network. Upon arriving at their rooms, patients were instructed to turn on their televisions that tuned automatically to "The Check-In Channel." The scripted program provided a welcome message and warm fuzzy overview of the facility, amenities, visitor policies, and other information geared to making hospital stays less stressful. In addition to putting patients at ease, the strategy shortened the admission process and cut administrative cost-per-patient by 20%!

Recommendation: Suggest the type of monitoring/level of care to be administered by the incoming shift. Examples:

- Routine care
- Need for urgent care
- Order change or referral to specialist

Now recognized as an essential best practice, the SBAR framework has fostered more accurate communications throughout medical staff and improved outcomes for hospital patients (source: ihi.org)[8].

Medicated Confusion

According to the National Academy of Medicine, more than 400,000 preventable drug-related injuries occur each year in hospitals. Another 800,000 occur in long-term care settings, and roughly 530,000 occur just among Medicare recipients in outpatient clinics. The organization's research committee estimates the cost to hospitals exceeds $3.5 billion annually before considering patient harm, lost wages, or other costs. (National Academy of Medicine, 7/20/2006.)

Drug naming, labeling, packaging, and dosage are primary contributors to medication errors across the board, including prescription drugs, over-the-counter products, vitamins, minerals, and herbal supplements. Outside the hospital, there are fewer safeguards available to prevent accidents, errors, and complications caused by the wrong drugs, too high a dosage or hazardous combinations.

Small, hard-to-read labels routinely lead to dangerous, inadvertent mistakes by professionals and consumers alike. Retail packaging also can be misleading. A pediatric study found that parents of infants routinely bought their infant's cough medicine that was formulated for children 13 months and older. The problem was traced to the packaging. The leading brands featured photos of babies who were well below the age specified as appropriate by the manufacturers. The parents assumed these medications were safe for all babies and did not check out the warning labels on the back. Fortunately, the side effects were not life-threatening.

That is not the case with hundreds of prescription medications that carry look-alike labels and have sound-alike names. The Food and Drug Administration receives more than 100,000 reports of dangerous medication errors each year. Bar code labels and electronic medical records systems are among the innovations introduced to address the issue, but these solutions are not universally available. The FDA also includes drug packaging in its review and approval process, but that, too, is not a foolproof preventative.

The drug industry and regulatory agencies have stepped up their communications and awareness efforts that target medical providers. The downside of this increased effort is more information overload ranging from notifications regarding changes in the strength of medications, updates to recommended dosages, new contraindications, and newly discovered hazardous combinations of medications

The Snake Oil Explosion

Outside the realm of legitimate medications is a parallel market that siphons off billions of healthcare dollars each year. Its origins trace back centuries through a long line of miracle cures preying upon those whose medical conditions defied known diagnosis. Initially, the popularity–and potential harm–of these counterfeit products was geographically limited depending on how fast the sheriff could run the traveling medicine show out of town. Now, it's an entirely new Wild West.

With the arrival of online advertising, what was once a cottage industry has exploded into a snake oil supernova. Each day, hundreds of millions of people are exposed to streams of digital ads for vitamins, minerals, herbs, oils, tonics, teas, serums, patches, and more that promise cures for every malady on earth. (Full disclosure, I have a client that develops and sells digestive enzyme formulations that I use myself.)

Fortune Business Insights estimates this global market will reach $128 billion by 2028, nearly double its current size[10]. Despite the lack of medically proven results for most of the products sold, huge sums of money will continue to fund this largely unregulated industry. Pseudo-scientific information makes up a significant portion of online marketing, capitalizing on the public's low rate of healthcare literacy. The digital Wild West will continue to be lucrative territory for sellers that leverage the cost of confusion into high-volume sales.

Off the Charts

According to the U.S. Centers for Medicaid and Medicare Services (source: CMS.govU.S. health care spending grew 2.7 percent in 2021, reaching $4.3 trillion or $12,914 per person. As a share of the nation's Gross Domestic Product, health spending accounted for 18.3 percent[11]. Given the examples highlighted in this section, it's not unreasonable to consider that confusion in this sector of the economy adds up to tens of millions of dollars in unnecessary costs per year. Every organization in the healthcare system can magnify its mission and lower costs simply by removing the potential for confusion at each patient touch point.

In a later chapter, I'll be describing a universal methodology for identifying and managing the risks that confusion presents to organizations, institutions, and businesses.

Author's Note

I began writing this book during Year Two of the Covid-19 global pandemic that has taken millions of lives and inflicted loss, hardship, and financial devastation worldwide. As I watched events unfold and witnessed the ever-shifting responses of political leaders, government agencies, trusted institutions, and public-facing experts, I realized the pandemic likely has generated the highest Cost of Confusion in human history. The failure to implement coherent communication strategies, provide consistent messaging and manage expectations realistically left a vacuum for misinformation. It is impossible to put a dollar amount on the losses or calculate what might have been avoided had leaders and health experts been prepared to control the narrative from Day One. If it seems likely that many public health experts are investigating this issue and writing about what can be learned and applied when next, we face a crisis of this magnitude. If not, then I know what my follow-up book needs to be.

Chapter 3

The Cost of Confusing Employees

BUT WHY?

If it's possible for two words to distill the driving principle of one's life, these are mine. They were not the first words I learned to speak, but they became the ones that accounted for most of the trouble I got myself into with parents, teachers, and, eventually, employers. It's not that I have a problem with authority. It's just that I expect authority to provide me with rational and credible reasons for carrying out orders. Well, a fella can dream...

I found myself writing this chapter last, perhaps, because of a deep personal connection to the topic. As a kid in a blue-collar neighborhood, I grew up at the tail end of the era in which the expectation was working for a big company until retirement (42 years in my father's case). With talent and luck, one could move steadily up the corporate ladder. Those who preferred a more predictable life could put in their decades of service in one department.

By the time I graduated from college, those were no longer default scenarios. Societal shifts and global economic forces have reshaped the dynamics of employment forever. Nevertheless, I managed to land a job in the audio-visual department of the country's largest life insurance company. Yet, it wasn't long before I realized that corporate life was not for me. It came down to those troublesome two words again—"but why?"

Asking that question about decisions, directives, and policies that affected our work was frowned upon. It wasn't so much that my bosses and coworkers *wouldn't* answer but that they *couldn't*. I began to appreciate how difficult it is for employees of sprawling corporations to genuinely grasp the whole nature of the business their employers are in. More difficult still is gaining a precise understanding of one's role and how exactly it contributes.

When I decided to set up Transform Communications, I followed the classic advice to write down a mission statement. Mine was "Celebrating

DOI: 10.4324/9781003301080-3

people in the work that they do." The choice of preposition was a deliberate one, reflecting my deep belief that work is the means through which we put our gifts in service to the world—while being compensated fairly for their value.

High-functioning organizations empower their people to do both.

Faint Signals

In contrast to the focus of other chapters, the Cost of Confusion inside an organization is more often diffused than direct. The primary impact is on overall productivity, and is reflected in myriad smaller metrics, e.g.:

Cycle Time	Production Costs	Warranty Claims
Error Rates	Quality	Employee Turnover
Rework	Rejection Rates	Fines And Litigation
Delays	Order Errors	
Decision Quality	Product Returns	

Each of these is an area in which deviations and trends (i.e., faint signals) can indicate that somebody, somewhere in the organization doesn't understand one or more aspects of their job. It can happen anywhere, at any level, and it drives down business performance. How much damage that inflicts depends on where the confusion is concentrated in the workforce and/or in the workflow. When negative effects extend to other people, functions, and departments, things add up until, at some point, we're talking real money.

Fortunately, there are strategies for proactively educating and engaging employees so that the Cost of Confusion begins to approach zero.

Paint the Big Picture

A good first step is ensuring that everyone in the organization has a fundamental understanding of the business. Sure, communicating *Mission, Vision, and Values* is important to building a strong organizational culture, but spelling out *Who We Are, Who We Serve, and What We Do* is critical to strong performance. Whether the company has ten employees or 10,000, each should be able to answer those three elemental questions. For extra credit, employees of for-profit enterprises should know how the company makes money or loses it and how their roles contribute to overall success.

At a minimum, these basics should be part of new employee orientation, but learning shouldn't stop there. Smart organizations continue pulling back the curtain to show employees how the gears turn. Overviews of business units, video tours of an assembly line, and customer interviews about how products or services contribute to their success—these are some of the communication options to help employees and other stakeholders feel they are part of something bigger.

There is also a deeper level of effectiveness that an organization can access when people gain greater insight into the roles and functions of their coworkers. Excellence doesn't happen in a vacuum. Consider what it takes for a professional football team to master a new play. Each of the 11 athletes on the field must understand his assignment relative to the other ten. Context is everything. Knowing which direction to go, when and how fast; what action to take in response to your opponent, adjusting to the unexpected—these are deeper levels of understanding that can benefit any group working toward a common goal—or goal line.

A Pact for Performance

Employers and employees frame their relationships legally through contracts, collective bargaining agreements, and other explicit terms. I believe there is an implicit agreement underlining the formal ones. Employers that expect employees to be dedicated to their jobs and shared success have an obligation to provide comprehensive support in six *Essential Knowledge Dimensions.*

THE **KNOW-WHAT**	Primary objectives, workflows, deliverables, tasks
THE **KNOW-WHO**	Interfaces with customers, partners, contributors /stakeholders
THE **KNOW-WHY**	Big picture business case & what's in it for them
THE **KNOW-HOW**	Processes, procedures, activities, interim steps
THE **KNOW-WITH**	Tools, templates, portals /systems/ applications
THE **KNOW-WHEN**	Timing: initiation, milestones, duration

Anyone who has ever worked in an organization can attest to the rarity of receiving and being empowered by knowledge in all six dimensions. The most common missing element is the WHY behind delegated responsibilities and expectations. Every dimension, however, is subject to missing or inadequate information and tools. To the extent that one or more of those knowledge dimensions is not addressed adequately and effectively, employee performance will suffer individually and collectively.

The chapter on Methodology goes into greater detail on how to assess, develop and deploy knowledge across these six dimensions. As a quick diagnostic tool, consider surveying how strongly individuals at every level in the organization would agree or disagree with the following statements:

1   I understand my job, and what is involved in performing it proficiently.
2   I know the internal and external roles that I serve/support.
3   I understand why my role is important to the success of the organization, and how that success impacts me personally.
4   I am knowledgeable about the processes and procedures my role requires.
5   I am equipped with the tools, technologies, and systems I need to excel in my job.
6   I have a clear sense of how long it takes to complete tasks and know when my expertise and work products must be delivered to others.

If a significant number of people "Strongly Disagree" with any of these statements, it is a good indication that people are receiving insufficient support in the corresponding knowledge category.

Blueprinting the Organization

Ford Motor Company gained notoriety for its slogan, "Quality is Job One." To be relevant in today's information economy, make that "Clarity is Job One." Clarity is the antidote to confusion and should be the desired state in every corner of an organization. Achieving that degree of clarity requires the organization to follow the ancient Greek aphorism, "Know Thyself."

Organizations seeking to operate at this high level of effectiveness conduct a rigorous intellectual inventory. Devoting time and resources to collecting, vetting, and organizing the accumulated historical knowledge provides the foundation from which clarity flows. Defining every job, clarifying its roles and responsibilities, and establishing the metrics to measure performance—this is the deep dive commitment that high-functioning organizations must make to eliminate vagueness and replace it with accountability. This level of due diligence won't turn employees into superstars, but it will ensure the are no more cracks for critical things to fall through.

As an organization develops its knowledge repository, the information is compiled in text-based documents distributed across digital libraries throughout the enterprise. To unlock the value of this information, employees must access, read, understand, and apply it proficiently. This can be a time-consuming process and a linear one. Along with those constraints, text-based knowledge also inhibits contributions from employees who are visual learners. The solution is to generate compelling graphics and imagery that illustrate key functions, major processes, primary technologies, and critical workflows. These visual frameworks help both types of learners—verbal and visual—gain a shared understanding of the business and a more meaningful context for their roles.

If a picture is worth a thousand words, the right information graphic is worth a thousand hours of productivity!

"It's All About the Margin"

By way of example, the accompanying illustration was designed to foster a sense of urgency for a strategic initiative to improve capital project management. Historically, the company had very little consistency around planning, engineering, and constructing its major refineries. Benchmarking against industry performance revealed that the company was spending $100 million more per year than its competitors did to execute a comparable set of projects. The typical response for most companies in that situation would be to increase prices and recoup some additional spending. Employees thought the same—and they were wrong.

The objective of the graphic was to illustrate that refining companies like theirs have no ability to control the cost of raw materials or to set the price at which their products are sold. External commodity markets determine both amounts. Therefore, to be profitable, the company must maximize the margin between what it pays for raw materials and what it receives when its products go to market. The four levers represent the things the company can control to improve its margins. In the case of the client's strategic initiative, all four levers would be pulled to drive profitability.

The ability to illustrate this story and other complex concepts was key to engaging the workforce. Individual employees began to contribute ideas, look beyond their silos, and bring other disciplines to the table earlier. What emerged was a collective willingness to adopt this new way of planning and executing projects. Over the next 24 months, projects became cost competitive with the rest of the industry. The $100 million overspend effectively became $100 million in savings to be reallocated to additional projects and increased capacity.

There is an art and a science to visualizing the inner workings of organizations. It generally does not involve PowerPoint and Visio—and should never include clip art! Because it is so readily available, clip art gets overused and misused. It is cheap, easy, and too often clichéd. This can lead

Commoditized Process Industry
It's all about the margin!

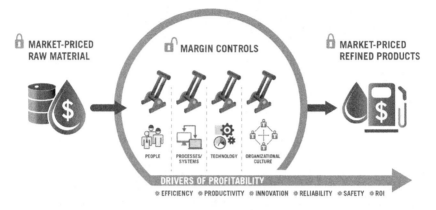

Figure 3.1

an audience to feel undervalued or to view the content as unimportant. In addition, relying on clip art can put important communications at risk. A piece of clip art inserted in one person's presentation might be used in a completely different context by the next person at the meeting.

Bottom line: if an organization has invested in a mission-critical initiative, it must make the investment in professionally produced visual communications. The same holds true for new employee onboarding and training, and development.

Along with professional graphic design, professional photo imagery is a vital component of visual communication for employees. The most powerful images are those pertaining directly to the organization. Ideal subjects include employees at work in their daily environments, candid interactions, products on the job in customer operations, and customer service scenes. The aim is to strengthen the kind of credibility and connection that comes from seeing relatable peers and recognizable situations.

For organizations without an in-house library of professional photos, stock photo libraries are viable alternatives. However, the same clip-art caveats apply for avoiding overused, clichéd, or too-cute photos. Images should be appropriate to the brand and carefully vetted for any errors or inconsistencies that can leave them vulnerable to criticism or ridicule.

I once fought a losing battle with a Big Three consulting firm over the hero image they selected for a client's corporate transformation initiative.

The photo featured a varsity rowing scull slicing through clear blue water, leaving a precise wake behind. The oars were perfectly synchronized, the rower's faces intent on their mission. Standing tall at the stern, the team coxswain (aka coach) held his megaphone high, barking the cadence. The problem with the photo? Everyone doing the rowing faces backward from the direction of travel. The photo failed completely as a visual metaphor for inspiring change. Instead, it reinforced the feeling employees had about being disregarded by leaders when it came to charting a course for the company. What's more, most college-educated employees graduated from Texas universities where varsity rowing was virtually unknown. Despite these flaws, the photo ended up on several print pieces and the cover slide of the PowerPoint template my design team, and I created for the initiative. And, yes, the image drew wisecracks from employees for months to come.

The Battle for Bandwidth

The 21st Century Information Economy has devolved into the Attention Economy. This is the digital pixel battlefield where media companies and advertisers vie moment to moment for the attention of hundreds of millions of content consumers. On screens of every size, the currency is eyeballs, measured in page views, likes, click-throughs, video plays, buy-now buttons, and other reflexive actions pushed by social media apps and the Internet.

In a world with so many digital stimuli, it is impossible for humans to process everything. The condition is known as Information Overload, the constant inundation of data that is characteristic of modern life. In response, many people have developed an adaptive superpower—the ability to TUNE OUT information that doesn't give them a compelling reason to pay attention to it. As content becomes bigger, brighter, bolder, faster, and louder, the modern workforce effectively is suspended between two extremes: Information Overload and Information Underwhelm.

The *overload* results from the sheer volume of information employees are expected to process daily, ranging from email correspondence to reports, instructions, spreadsheets, webinars, and more. When a system overloads, it shuts down. Humans have a similar response, one that impairs cognitive function, inhibits productivity, and compromises the quality of their work.

The *underwhelm* results from the bland uniformity of information used in the workplace. The world runs on billions of pages of electronic documents housed in sprawling shared libraries. Little effort goes into making them easy or engaging to use. For a generation of employees that consume a steady stream of addictive digital entertainment, it is difficult to excel in roles that deal with dense, dull, and mind-numbing content every day.

To motivate a workforce stuck between confusion and complacency, enterprise organizations must adapt to shorter attention spans. This requires innovative thinking about the ways critical information is packaged and delivered to employees. There are at least three ways to achieve this goal:

- Increase the rate of knowledge transfer by delivering more information in less time
- Boost comprehension levels companywide through the use of powerful information graphics, conversational language, and advanced learning models
- Leverage the value of expert knowledge by engaging each stakeholder audience on its own terms, where it sits in the business

To address and obtain higher thresholds of engagement, a critical first step is to begin managing employees' daily information diet for better nutrition. In many organizations, intranets display information without meaningful visual architecture. The corporate main page resembles a break room bulletin board. There is a grid, but topics appear in a random fashion. They range from employee blood drive, community volunteer opportunities, and safety moments to windows displaying the stock price, recent promotions, AND news on strategic corporate initiatives. It's all the news that fits on the screen, competing for employees' attention and mindshare.

High-performance organizations take charge of what their intranets broadcast to employees. The important companywide initiatives get top billing and more home screen real estate to keep business objectives front and center.

It's Lonely at The Top—and Confusing Too

None of the preceding topics is intended to suggest that the confusion is occurring inside an organization only flows downhill. Confusion at the top of an organization is just as likely and potentially more costly. The larger the organization, the wider the chasm is between executives and front-line workers. That means a greater risk of major disconnects between those setting the strategy and those responsible for implementing it.

Then, there is the underlying dynamic that comes with the territory of working for an organization— effectively being told how to do your job by someone who may have little or no idea about what your job entails. This is where the age-old battle lines between Us and Them are drawn. Unless a leader comes "up through the ranks," he or she can never know exactly what happens on the shop floor, along the assembly line, or at the sales counter.

The accumulated knowledge of the front-line workforce comes from hands-on experience. These everyday experts grasp what makes the gears turn: processes, procedures, nuanced protocols, practical considerations, technology limitations, resource constraints, interdependencies, and many more intricacies that executive leadership teams can fail to comprehend. Without clear understanding of the inner workings of their organizations, leaders can make classic "out-of-touch" mistakes: overpromising to shareholders and external stakeholders, setting unrealistic targets for productivity, revenue, and growth, and imposing practices and procedures that make jobs more difficult, not less.

Smart organizations don't make those mistakes. The smartest ones recognize the importance of front-line experience, knowledge, and expertise. To capture their value, these organizations have mechanisms in place to bring workforce knowledge early on into high-level planning and decision-making. This can prevent executive decision-makers from committing to an investment or a course of action that is untenable.

Perhaps the most notable example is the global automaker VW. The company's works council represents a commitment to social partnership and co-determination. The works council is made up of representatives from different departments and levels of the organization, who are elected by their fellow employees. It functions like a traditional labor union to participate in setting pay and benefits, working conditions, and training programs. Where the council differs from a union is that it has an actual "seat at the table" with direct involvement in corporate decision-making[12]. (Washington Post, 2/10/2014.)

The works council members on the VW supervisory board contribute workforce insight and have voting rights on high-level business decisions such as major investments, mergers and acquisitions, and changes to the company's strategy. This ensures that line-level and mid-level employees' interests, knowledge, and concerns are considered when the company is making decisions that impact the entire organization.

Another practice for leveraging workforce knowledge at VW is the use of cross-functional teams. These bring together representatives from different departments and levels of the organization to work on specific projects or initiatives. These teams can be tasked with identifying key strategic priorities for the company and then developing and implementing plans to achieve those goals. This consistent capacity to align efforts within and across its global organization has enabled Volkswagen Group to be a dominant force in the auto-making industry, consistently ranking #2 in sales after Japan's Toyota.

Not all responses have to be so comprehensive as those at VW. For smaller organizations, simply narrowing the chasm between the highest and lowest levels of employees can increase clarity, lead to more innovation, and enable faster response. Many companies in the high-tech outdoor apparel sector are recognized for being early adopters of the so-called flattened organizational structure. This involves reducing the number of management layers overall, thus moving line employees and decision-makers closer together on the organization chart. In real-world terms, this means shorter and more direct lines of communication and feedback. By encouraging employees to share their knowledge and ideas, respected brands like Gore-Tex, Patagonia, The North Face and others have established cultures of innovation that drive development of new products[13].

Along with reducing confusion, development from the bottom up tends to be faster than its opposite. Early participation of line-level employees surfaces the obstacles and challenges associated with manufacturing so that new designs can get into production sooner and on the market quicker. In the reverse mode, designers and engineers create cool stuff first and then send their concepts to the manufacturing division to figure out how to produce them. Invariably, that approach takes longer and determines how quickly new products get to market.

> "The most successful leaders understand they must win the hearts and minds of employees in a way that is true, authentic, and real. If you get those human components right, the performance of the system can work. Without them, you're nowhere."
> — Keith Yamashita, Founder, SYPartners
> (WSJ, 5/13/2002)[14]

Technology: Why More Is Not Always Better

It's the universal promise of every new workplace technology: more productivity. Some go one step further to add "with fewer employees," but the claims are the same—enabling people to work smarter, faster, more accurately, and ultimately, more cost effectively. Missing from that list is "more miserably." That may be an overstatement, but it warrants considering the tradeoffs and unintended consequences that are part of every technology "advance."

The Persistent Myth of Multi-Tasking

When the modern digital workplace arrived, everybody was multi-tasking, or so we thought. Scan the inbox while typing a memo and talking on the phone—no problem. In truth, those actions were not simultaneous. They relied on our brain's ability to emulate a high-speed switch, instantly shifting our focus from each task to the next and back again. In the early 2000s, research finally debunked the myth. There is no such thing as multitasking.

That freed people to work on one thing at a time, without guilt and, seemingly, with greater productivity. Turns out that was a myth, too. Attention spans and productivity are directly linked. Any disruption to the former decreases the latter. It's cognitive whiplash.

According to Cal Newport, computer-science professor, and author of *Deep Work*, "What we didn't realize is that even when you jump over to check the inbox and come right back, it can be just as damaging as multitasking. When you looked at that email inbox for 15 seconds, you initiated a cascade of cognitive changes." (NYT, 1/22/23)[15]

> *"Deep Work is a professional activity performed in a state of distraction-free concentration that pushes your cognitive capabilities to their limit. These efforts create new value, improve your skill, and are hard to replicate."*— Cal Newport[15]

Email is but one distraction for a workforce now using suites of digital tools designed to improve focus and efficiency. Adding to that challenge is the skyrocketing amount of collaboration being done remotely using platforms designed to seamlessly connect colleagues anywhere in the world. Accomplishing "Deep Work" within this hyper-connected context is a daunting challenge.

The average white-collar employee is a slave to technology. A tsunami of email, plus time spent instant messaging, juggling remote-meeting apps, and feeding data into workflow and project-management software, leaves little time for the tasks that are generated. Instead of having a handle on work, many employees feel like they are drowning in it. Newport explains why.

"The critical mindset shift is understanding that even minor context shifts are productivity poison. So, if you have to work on something cognitively demanding, the rule has to be zero context shifts during that period." (NYT, 1/23/22)[15]

When organizations closed their offices in response to the pandemic and sent employees to work from home, a more abrupt shift began. People ramped up their use of the very technologies that drive context shifts. Hyperactive messaging apps like Slack created a continuous flow of back-and-forth distractions and context shifts. When not reading chats and typing replies, the brain maintains a heightened level of vigilance for the next pop-up or inbox alert. The expectation these apps create is for an immediate response, making it difficult for employees to ignore notifications or turn them off for significant chunks of time.

There are no quick and easy answers. Research is widespread among social scientists, organizational experts, neuropsychologists, and many more specialists to understand the implications for the human brain, digital communication, and collaborative workflow. It's a landscape ripe with possibilities for creating costly confusion.

For now, some productivity experts suggest going "old school" by picking up the phone (or web meeting equivalent) to converse one on one in real-time. A handful of brief, focused calls over the course of the workday may replace as many as 50 or 60 text chats and emails between two people, according to Cal Newport.

Stop The Madness (of Meetings)

Another consequence of the pandemic was an out-of-control explosion in online group meetings. As the leading technology enabler (or culprit), Microsoft Corporation compiled data on how its business software suite was used as the effects of Covid-19 rippled through the nationwide workforce. Between February 2020 and February 2022, research revealed that the number of Microsoft Teams meetings per week more than *doubled* for the average user. During that same two-year period, the amount of time Teams users spent in meetings more than *tripled*. (WSJ, 2/1/23)[16]

With in-person interaction a thing of the past, managers turned to more frequent department meetings to keep track of what their teams were doing. Employees invited their colleagues to meetings as a way of increasing visibility. Executives scheduled more virtual Town Halls and All-Hands meetings as a tactic to keep their people connected to the mission.

Not surprisingly, employees reported that a large percentage of the online meetings they were required to attend provided no meaningful business value. As meeting calendars became fully booked day in and day out, employees had less and less time to accomplish the work expected of them. This led, in part, to the wave of burned-out remote workers who left the workforce voluntarily in what HR experts called "The Great Resignation."

It was a tipping point for many organizations. They realized meetings were out of control, and some leaders began taking drastic action. Shopify, an eCommerce platform provider, decided to make a bold move in early January of 2023. It deleted 12,000 scheduled events from employees' calendars. According to the company, that move freed up an estimated 95,000 staff hours for the year. (WSJ, 2/1/23)[16] Seems reasonable to expect those hours will translate into a dramatic boost in productivity. Another potential benefit is reducing burnout and turnover among Shopify's workforce.

Many other companies are taking steps to claw back the excessive amount of time their employees have lost to "meeting madness." Instituting a weekly "no-meeting day" allows people to plan on at least one full day of uninterrupted work time. That still may not be enough to manage the work that stacks up during the other four days of meetings, but it's a start.

Other organizations are looking at hard stop times, more focused agendas, and dialing back on the number of people invited. The average number of online meetings may never return to pre-pandemic levels, but the out-of-control madness is responding to treatment.

Tag Teams: Asynchronous Work

Before closing this section on the dark side of technology, one more round of myth-busting is warranted. The subject: asynchronous work. The term refers to remote work that is done by teams whose individual members do not collaborate simultaneously. In other words, they work without being online at the same time. Effectively, asynchronous work is the opposite of real-time collaboration by teams using Slack or other instant messaging apps and online meetings.

Promoters of asynchronous work contend that it accelerates the delivery of projects and helps companies move faster than competitors. While many tech companies have embraced the idea and made the model work for them, it may not be a fit for the workflows of organizations in other industry sectors. The question is will an asynchronous work mode be faster or just create the illusion of speed?

In the case of teams that are globally distributed across multiple time zones, one member's workday may be another member's middle of the night. The inability to align members' schedules forces teams to communicate exclusively through ongoing review and comment cycles, extended email threads, and other internal channels. Moving a project forward gets bogged down by the wait for all comments to come in, and then more time is spent circulating them all again for further discussion. When the group reaches a consensus on the revisions, someone implements the changes, and the new version gets cycled yet again to secure signoffs. Only then does a deliverable move on to the next stage of development or to another part of the organization.

There is ample room for debate over speed and productivity, but what asynchronous work cannot leverage is team synergy. The best and biggest breakthroughs happen when the right people interact as a group in real-time. This is where the magic happens. Historically, breakthroughs are associated with putting people into one room to hash out a complex problem from every angle. While face-to-face interaction remains the proven approach, game-changing ideas can and do come out of online meetings. Live interaction inspires passion and excitement in ways that asynchronous work cannot match. Tag teaming good ideas across 12 time zones can result in better ideas but rarely will it produce great ones.

How Organizations Confuse Themselves

The chapter began with a focus on confusion at the micro level, i.e., the impact on individual employees. There also is a macro level at which confusion operates. Things that routinely happen inside of organizations can drain business value without anyone noticing. The impacts can ripple through entire departments and business divisions, undermine strategies, and lead to very bad decisions.

Often, when organizations confuse themselves, the root cause is a failure in governance.

Governance is a framework of policies, codes, rules, and procedures that ensure prudent management. Governance seeks to eliminate ambiguity and confusion by providing clear lines of authority to prevent abuses of power and control. By defining all roles, delineating their responsibilities, and making accountability explicit, governance imposes order and establishes boundaries within the workforce. Other components of governance prescribe how major decisions are made and the degree of participation and transparency required. Simply put, governance attempts to keep organizations from doing stupid stuff. Obviously, this is not a foolproof solution.

Thanks to long-term relationships with a handful of large corporations, I have witnessed a fair share of train wrecks. In almost every case, the reasons why things went off the rails came down to governance or lack thereof. Perhaps, it was the absence of disciplined processes to govern decision-making and manage large-scale endeavors. When these frameworks did exist, it was a failure to adhere to them that led to fiasco. Somewhere in the organization, one or more people decided the rules didn't apply to them.

Breach of Process

One example comes from among my energy sector clients. It began with the announcement of the company's first international project, a new LNG (Liquid Natural Gas) production plant to be built on the coast of Mexico. The project organization was assembled and fully staffed, estimates completed, and the engineering contractor ramped up to full capacity. One lone voice on the project team pointed out that the lease for the site had not been finalized. Not only that, but no other site met all the criteria required to make the project economically feasible. Unless the plant was built on that specific site, it would never be profitable.

Nevertheless, it was full speed ahead on the project for the engineering contractor and for procurement of major components. The red flag regarding the site would be ignored for more than 18 months until the business development team admitted to the failure of negotiations with the Mexican government. The site was not going to be leased, ever. The project was canceled abruptly after having spent more than $200 million on engineering alone.

This trainwreck was completely avoidable. If the project's executive sponsor and team had followed the company's established project process, all work and associated spending would have been halted until the site was secured.

When the stakes are high, by-passing critical steps in the capital project development process should never be allowed. To do so is a failure of governance.

New Sheriff in Town

In a variation on that theme, organizations tend to overlook the disruption and confusion that accompany the hiring or promotion of senior executives and high-level managers. This is especially true when the new person comes from outside the organization. Through a combination of ego and temperament, many of these leaders are convinced they need to come in and immediately shake things up. They want everyone to know there is a new sheriff in town. Instead of taking the time to understand how well the town has been running under his predecessor, the new sheriff summarily dismisses long-standing conventions. Sometimes, that is exactly what the town—and the organization—need. Just as often, however, the status quo is a sound place to start.

Workplace cultures that allow this behavior to go unchallenged risk alienating employees and undermining the hard-won value of processes and procedures that have proved their worth. The gears can grind to a halt while everyone in the sheriff's organization is trying to figure out what is expected of them.

High-performing organizations have figured out how to minimize this kind of disruption. First, they use the hiring process to screen for leaders who have the humility, insight, and maturity to step thoughtfully into their new roles. Then, as new executives are hired (or promoted internally), there is a comprehensive onboarding process to provide each leader with a nuanced overview of the organization he or she will be leading. With a clear understanding of what has been working and what needs to be improved, the new sheriff won't have to arrive with guns blazing.

Tardy to the Party: The Late-Arriving Decision Maker

This pitfall is a variation on the theme of allowing personality to trump process. In this scenario, the organization has an important decision to make. It could involve a major acquisition, a seven-figure technology investment, a capital construction project, or another endeavor requiring a commitment of money and resources.

Typically, the organization's governance includes a designated process for making decisions like these. The process starts by assembling a qualified small group to conduct extensive research, consider potential options, and recommend the most prudent course of action. This is known as performing due diligence.

The most robust processes involve the primary decision makers early on to gain their input, outline the approach, and agree on the scope and parameters. It is not unusual for these executives to skip this part of the process. The reasons vary. Sometimes, schedules and commitments prevent decision-makers from participating. Sometimes, executives choose not to participate. This sets the stage for them to become "late-arriving decision makers."

These are leaders who have neither contributed to the due diligence effort nor monitored its progress. Consequently, they are unaware of how much information has been refined and how much seasoned expertise has been added. As the term declares, late-arriving decision makers show up at or near the end of the process. One of two things happens next.

One—the executive acknowledges the value that has been "baked into" the group's recommendations. After review, discussion, and clarifying questions, the decision maker proceeds to decide the outcome.

Two—the executive wants everything laid out in detail, starting from the beginning. In rare instances, the late-arriving decision maker may add a crucial piece of new information not available to the group earlier. It may or may not change their recommendations.

The leader may order the group to recycle its process and generate additional information to get support for the decision he or she already has made. At this late stage, rework typically does not correlate with making a better decision.

Whether or not late-arriving decision makers agree with the recommendations or make a completely different decision, the message to employees is the same. Certain people in positions of authority are exempt from abiding by the organization's governing processes. The takeaway for line employees is, "Why bother." This attitude may impair decision quality permanently unless all of the leadership is held accountable to governance processes.

Golden Rules: Symptoms Not Solutions

It is common to see top-down decrees issued by executive teams frustrated with organizational performance. When they can't put their finger on exactly what is causing the problem, some leaders opt for the broadbrush approach known as the golden rules. Everyone knows the original Golden Rule:

Do Unto Others as You Would Have Them Do Unto You.

In organizations, golden rules are a set of simple-to-understand principles designed to encourage desired behaviors linked to business performance.

Conventional wisdom considers golden rules to be solutions. What if golden rules are symptoms? The decision to introduce a set of golden rules can indicate an underlying problem that has not been fully identified and understood. The issues could be the result of inadequate management systems, misaligned objectives, or the workplace culture. When it comes to deep-seated issues, golden rules provide little, if any, positive contributions to the task of resolving the problem. Consider this example.

A management consulting team completed an exhaustive root cause analysis and lessons learned report for a global project organization. Following a discussion of the findings and next steps, the organization's executive leader began drafting a set of golden rules. He determined that nine rules were needed to address the identified shortcomings of his organization. (As golden rules go, three is optimum, and seven still works. But nine? At that point, why not add one more and call them "commandments?")

As a member of the consulting team, I was curious to understand the deeper issues involved. This led me to reread our team's reports to look for any correlation between the problems' root causes and the project management system the company had rolled out two years earlier.

I expected to find gaps and tools missing that would account for the root cause findings. Instead, I found a one-to-one link between each root cause and a specific component of the system that existed to prevent it. In other words, the management system had a defined process or a tool that precluded the need for any of the nine golden rules. The root cause issues were not system related. They were application related. Project teams did not fully and properly use the prescribed process and tools at their disposal. Some teams did not develop the full set of required work plans. Other teams bypassed quality reviews. Due to inadequate project controls, the organization's projects were over budget and behind schedule.

The discovery that all problems were due to lapses in teams' application of management processes and tools had, in effect, made the nine golden rules superfluous. Project teams lacked nothing. They had access to everything they needed to manage their projects. With just a little more targeted training, teams could begin to apply the process effectively and improve project performance. There was no reason to add golden rules to the mix.

Despite our contention, the golden rules were unnecessary (and confusing), they were issued with great fanfare. Project teams got a new set of management directives added to their plates. No big deal—maybe. There are unintended consequences to consider. By elevating the nine golden rules, the organization risks neutralizing its more robust systems and processes. The message that teams take away is, "Hey if we just follow the golden rules, we're golden!"

Even if they are carved in stone, golden rules alone can't take the place of robust project management systems and teams that know how to use them.

Don't Call Them "Lessons Learned"*

Every large corporate client I have worked with has promoted the importance of lessons learned. Some client organizations go so far as to invest time and resources in the exercise upon completion of every project. The purpose is to capture, review, and summarize things that went wrong and describe how the team responded to fix them. Generally included is advice to future teams on how to avoid repeating mistakes. This is a noble endeavor. The problem lies in what happens next.

After their initial release, lessons learned are filed away and forgotten. After seeing some of the same mistakes repeated over the years, I believe "lessons learned" should be renamed "lessons identified." Whether they are "learned" depends on what the organization does with the knowledge behind each lesson.

If lessons identified remain buried in some abandoned archive, there is little to no chance they will be discovered and used to benefit future teams. Of course, lessons can travel as living memory, carried by team members moving from a completed project to one just getting started. The knowledge remains transient, however, and leaves with people exiting the organization.

One partially effective tactic is to compile all lessons in an easily accessible database. This captures them permanently but is missing a mechanism to leverage their value. That mechanism is behavior!

It works like this. Simply require every project team to both use and contribute to the database—and incentivize that behavior. In other words, using and contributing lessons identified is factored into performance reviews and financial bonuses. To ensure the behavior takes place, a designated member of the team is assigned responsibility for managing lessons-learned activities.

Beware of These Hidden Costs of Confusion!

Ten examples of hidden costs that can arise when organizations fail to communicate clearly:

1 Loss of employee productivity, as employees may struggle to understand their jobs and the company's goals and priorities.
2 Increased costs of training and onboarding, as new employees may struggle to understand the company's processes and culture.
3 Increased risk of security breaches due to employee confusion and failure to adhere to cybersecurity policies and procedures.
4 Loss of morale and engagement, as employees may become frustrated or disillusioned with a company that is perceived as lacking direction or undervaluing their contributions.
5 Increased customer support costs, as confused customers may require more assistance in understanding the company's products or services.
6 Loss of customer trust and loyalty, leading to decreased sales and revenue.
7 Increased risk of legal action, as confused communications may lead to misunderstandings and disputes with customers, partners, or regulators.
8 Damage to the company's reputation, as confusing communications may make the company appear unreliable or untrustworthy.
9 Loss of opportunities, as potential partners or investors may be hesitant to engage with a company that is perceived as disorganized and lacking a coherent message.
10 Loss of competitive advantage to competitors that communicate more effectively with their potential customers.

Here is a suggested sequence for implementation.

1. Designated team member reviews the database for potentially applicable lessons and presents an initial set to the team.
2. Team reaches a consensus on the specific lessons to apply.

3. Team and manager agree on the selected lessons.
4. Team documents application of lessons over the course of their assignment
5. At close of project, team members develop their own lessons learned and submit for review and inclusion in the database.
6. Upon completion of steps 1-5, team members share a bonus (predetermined by the organization) with an extra amount going to the designated coordinator.

Putting the above into practice will vary according to the nature of the assignments. Each organization will determine the minimum number of lessons learned to be selected from its database and the number to be contributed by teams at closeout.

For decades, lessons learned exercises have delivered only a fraction of their business value. Making this organizational, cultural, and financial commitment provides the key to unlocking the rest of that value.

Author reserves the right to include a pet peeve

When Smart People Make Bad Decisions

For their sheer dollar value, nothing says "Cost of Confusion" like failed mergers and acquisitions. America's corporate landscape is dotted with them. Some fizzled fast. Others took a few years. Some should never have happened. Still, others were victims of failure to execute. Here are brief examples highlighting how confusion and lack of understanding led to costly mistakes referred to euphemistically as "making a bad bet."

AT&T's acquisition of DirecTV. In 2015, AT&T acquired DirecTV for $49 billion. The deal was aimed at expanding AT&T's presence in the video market and providing it with a national satellite TV platform to bundle with its mobile phone packages. What AT&T's due diligence failed to capture was the steep rise of streaming services. The timing of the deal could not have been worse. AT&T made its purchase at the tipping point of pay-TV's decline. The telecommunications giant also struggled to integrate DirecTV's operations. Service suffered, and customer complaints skyrocketed. Since the deal closed, AT&T has been unable to stem the exodus of millions of subscribers in recent years. Adding to the challenges is the high debt load that has limited investment in new technology and services.

Microsoft's acquisition of Nokia. In 2014, Microsoft acquired Nokia's phone business for $7.2 billion. The deal was aimed at helping Microsoft to gain a foothold in the smartphone market and better compete with Apple and Google. However, the acquisition was plagued by problems. Many stemmed from Microsoft's failure to understand the competitive nature of the smartphone market. As a company that completely dominates its market sector, Microsoft struggled to integrate Nokia's operations. Other challenges arose in navigating the differences in organizational culture that existed between the American and Finnish teams. The acquisition was viewed as a failure among the technology and investor communities. Just a year later, Microsoft opted to write down the value of the Nokia business by $7.6 billion and lay off thousands of employees.

AT&T's merger with Time Warner Media. Talks began between AT&T and Time Warner Media in 2016, aimed at creating a media and telecommunications giant. AT&T would provide the distribution network (including DirectTV). Time Warner would provide a steady supply of media content from its holdings, HBO, Warner Bros., CNN, and Turner. At the outset, the merger was opposed by regulatory agencies. Others criticized the powerhouse combination, fearing it would lead to increased prices for consumers and reduced competition in the media industry. Despite the hurdles, the parties won approval to close the deal. In 2018, AT&T formally acquired Time Warner Media for $85 billion.

Repeating the mistakes of its past acquisitions, AT&T struggled to integrate Time Warner's operations. It was a clash of cultures—telecommunications versus creatives. At the end of 2020, just two years after the merger, the company was forced to write down the value of the merged assets by $3.5 billion.

In 2022, with restructuring still incomplete, the leadership team acknowledged that AT&T had "made a bad bet." The strategy to dismantle the media conglomerate involved a spin-off of WarnerMedia for a new merger with Discovery. Thus far, AT&T has recouped only $43 billion of its original $85 billion investment.

As the media and entertainment sector grapples with post-pandemic shifts and corporate reshuffling, the shakeout and the fallout continue. Expect more failed mergers, acquisitions, and spin-offs before the dust settles.

These three Cost of Confusion examples highlight the absolute importance of understanding the nature of the business being acquired. This means knowing exactly why the business has been successful, how its market works, and what makes it desirable to own. The range of factors to research relentlessly includes products and services, culture, technology, key relationships, competitors, and, of course, financial performance.

Based on that understanding, the acquiring company must think in terms of Benefits Realization before actively pursuing its target. This involves a 360-degree examination to understand everything needed to maintain the operating integrity of its purchase. What are the critical capabilities that keep the gears turning and the revenue flowing? Who are the key people to support and motivate? In addition to short-term benefits realization, new owners need an actionable strategic plan to increase the value of the asset over the long term.

The work that takes place after a deal closes has even more riding on it than the effort that preceded it. Confusion permeates each discrete organization that comes together, whether through a merger or an acquisition. High-level talks and decisions will have cascading impacts on the balance of the workforce. There is urgency and intensity about the integration of systems, processes, and cultures.

And everything is taking place in an atmosphere of fear and uncertainty. Employees are wondering about job security as well as how their jobs will change, who they will report to, and what the new expectations will be. The full gamut of Cost of Confusion indicators will be on display: decreased productivity, quality control problems, spikes in customer service complaints, and many more.

It bears repeating this table that appears at the beginning of the chapter. It is obligatory to provide full support in these *Essential Knowledge Dimensions* during and after a merger or acquisition. All employees are owed nothing less.

THE **KNOW-WHAT**	Primary objectives, workflows, deliverables, tasks
THE **KNOW-WHO**	Interfaces with customers, partners, contributors /stakeholders
THE **KNOW-WHY**	Big picture business case & what's in it for them
THE **KNOW-HOW**	Processes, procedures, activities, interim steps
THE **KNOW-WITH**	Tools, templates, portals /systems/ applications
THE **KNOW-WHEN**	Timing: initiation, milestones, duration

(**NOTE:** Readers who anticipate being involved in a fast-approaching merger or acquisition should jump ahead to Chapter 9, Methodology. The process and tools there will be helpful to understanding, navigating, and adding value during the transition.)

What Were They Thinking??

As the prior examples of missing or inadequate governance illustrate, flawed decision making is another way that organizations can confuse themselves. The money-losing deals cited here indicate that executive leaders and board members either overlooked warning signals or failed to understand something crucial about their target acquisitions. As a result, smart people made bad decisions.

Historically, proposed deals get put together by the Mergers & Acquisitions department. Then, it becomes the job of senior executives to "sell" the board of directors on the vision. The inherent flaw in this approach is that it often results in an inadequate understanding of risks and precludes looking at alternatives, including "hard pass."

In contrast, the concept of Decision Quality turns the process into a collaborative one. Parties agree in advance on the decision to be made and identify the types and scope of information needed to provide the appropriate degree of due diligence. Setting the parameterstogether established shared ownership of major decisions. More important, it increases the probability that the decision made will achieve all desired business outcomes for the organization.

The Decision Quality Diagram is a simple but powerful tool groups use to determine whether they are adequately prepared to decide or if more work must be done. Also called the Spider Diagram by virtue of its webbed shape, the tool displays the six attributes of decision quality.

Decision Quality

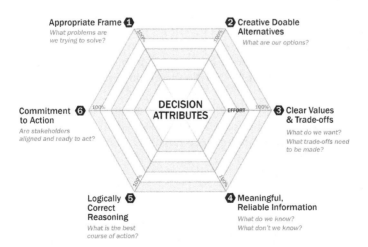

Figure 3.2

Before making a decision, the preparation team and the decision makers do a self-assessment of their efforts in each attribute. Using the scale along each axis, the group agrees on a percentage (between zero and 100%) that reflects the level of development. A dot is placed on each axis to indicate the percentage score. When all six attributes have been scored, a line is drawn to connect each dot. This creates the "spider diagram," a visual representation of overall decision quality. Generally, the diagram should be relatively balanced, with all scores in the 60-70% range. Any weak scoring attributes are easy to see and must be addressed before making the decision. Balance is the objective, as inadequacy in any one attribute degrades the overall quality of the decision.

Coincidentally, researchers studying the "science" of decision-making have concluded that the 80/20 Rule applies here. Decision quality peaks at attribute scores of 80%. Putting time and resources toward that last 20% on the diagram has no measurable impact. Statistically, decisions made with 80% scores on each attribute turned out just as well as decisions made with higher scores.

In my book, organizations that subject their employees to competing agendas, conflicting messages, and contradictory orders need better leaders—leaders with a commitment to clarity. They recognize that clarity provides the surest path to shared success. These leaders instill clarity of purpose from the top down. They understand that asking people to do great work depends on providing employees with a critical understanding of their roles and the support they need to contribute every day.

Big or small, employers have an obligation to provide the right information at the right level of detail to the right people at the right time. Employees, in turn, have a responsibility to pay attention, process the information, and apply it as intended as they perform their assigned tasks.

The nature and amount of information will vary according to the size of the organization and the type of business it's in, but the objective remains the same: cutting the Cost of Confusion to empower performance.

"When you're clear, everyone can be on the same page, everyone can contribute their maximum and do their best, and everyone knows where things stand." — Ann Latham, *The Power of Clarity*[17]

Chapter 4

The Cost of Confusing Citizens

I honestly don't know where to start... since the dawn of civilization, governing institutions have been innately driven to overcomplicate everything they touch. Layers of bureaucracy, siloed organizations, conflicting agendas, and competing constituencies are a few of the causal factors at work. Although bold prescriptions are outside the scope of this book (and the intellectual capacity of the author), there is value in considering how policies, legislation, regulations, and more create widespread confusion throughout the body politic. Making political leaders and public sector employees aware of the ways in which government creates confusion opens up the possibility for change. This chapter explores breaking the cycle of frustration that citizens experience and raising the bar on the government's capacity to improve the lives of those it serves.

The DEQ Surprise

Sorry—not an ice cream treat. The snappy title refers to an additional $25 fee that drivers discovered when renewing their auto registration in the state of Oregon. This customer service failure was taking place daily at checkout counters inside emissions testing stations operated by the Oregon Department of Air Quality.

The process begins when owners receive their registration renewal notices by mail every two years. The notice references vehicle information and states the applicable fee. Also mentioned is the need for an additional document certifying that the vehicle has passed the DEQ emissions inspection. For decades that meant two separate trips—one to an inspection site and one to the Department of Motor Vehicles. Fortunately, that was simplified eventually by setting up DEQ stations to issue renewal stickers to owners upon completion of the emissions test. This created a one-stop shop experience but a two-cost transaction. That is when the unpleasantness began.

DOI: 10.4324/9781003301080-4

Seeing their cars pass the test, owners stepped up to the counter and handed over their checks for the cost of registration (credit cards not accepted) only to be informed that they owed $25 more for the DEQ test fee. Invariably, there was sticker shock (pun intended) and the need for state employees to explain the additional charge to their suddenly very disgruntled customers.

I personally encountered this situation and, during one of my subsequent trips, asked the counter person how often he had to explain the extra amount each day. He told me there were days when it was every other person. Off the top of my head, I suggested adding an explanation to the registration notices so that people would not be surprised when they stepped up to the checkout counter. I cannot claim the credit, but my next renewal notice contained an additional strip of paper explaining that I should expect to pay an additional $25 when renewing registration at a DEQ station.

The DEQ Surprise is just one example of the tens of millions of interactions taking place daily in city, county, state, and federal offices across the country. From building permits, dog licenses, new business registration, and myriad other administrative functions, public bureaucracies often fail to recognize how convoluted their processes are. Information handoffs and internal approvals are complicated and not always clear to those responsible for issuing formal documents. Consequently, citizens typically must make multiple trips in person or repeated visits to online portals to conclude their business.

For now, the only option is old-fashioned relationship building—find a person in some corner of the bureaucracy who still cares about the level of service members of the public receive. Making a personal connection is a strategy I have used successfully for years, but it's not a true solution.

In a confusion-free world, government entities would map out their top transactional processes to delineate the key parties, sequence of steps, and required information involved at each step. That exercise has the advantage of educating internal providers about the efficacy of their typical business processes as well as revealing potentially redundant or unnecessary steps.

Development of visual roadmaps depicting each service provider's processes, players, and steps can ensure that citizens of every stripe will have the most time-efficient and effective interaction possible. Application of analytical tools also can improve processes continually. Online metrics such as visitor counts, click streams, overall time onsite data and rates of abandoned payments are vital data points. Together, they determine how long the average user spends on the services portal and indicate whether the person was successful in completing the transaction for a new license, permit, or traffic violation in an efficient manner.

Outside the digital realm, similar metrics can reveal the median number of interactions needed to complete a task and the time spent filling out forms or sitting in waiting rooms. Time efficiency is the key. Public agencies that reduce overall transaction time for citizens to achieve their desired outcomes will increase the public's satisfaction with their government services.

When Good Policy Flops

History is littered with policy innovations that have failed to deliver on their potential to improve lives. One that is still being explained periodically during the two-plus decades since its passage is the Health Savings Account (HSA). Described as the IRAs of the insurance world, HSAs are an attempt by Congress to encourage individuals to build up savings for healthcare and withdraw money tax-free when needed to pay for medical expenses.

What makes the HSA unique among federally created saving vehicles is that it is the consummate "free lunch" for taxpayers. Contributions, account growth, and withdrawals—are TAX-FREE, so long as the withdrawals are used for specified medical costs. The other requirement to set up an HSA is a high deductible health insurance policy. This type of policy offer significantly lower monthly premiums to offset the risk of incurring greater out-of-pocket costs in any given year. The reasoning is that participants can invest those premium savings in their HSA while taking advantage of the tax-free compound growth. On a broader policy angle, the idea was that giving people greater control over their healthcare spending would put pressure on costs and foster competition among insurance providers.

Sounds like a no-brainer, right? Unfortunately, participation rates have lagged projections since the program launched more than 20 years ago. Much of the confusion stems from the high-deductible insurance component. Consumers are frightened by the prospect of larger deductible amounts than they would experience under traditional employer-sponsored plans. What gets lost in poor translation is that the likelihood of the person actually having to pay that high maximum deductible year after year is very small. People react to the looming big number and do not understand the relationship between risk and probability.

HSA plans are marketed by a wide range of professionals, including insurance brokers, accountants, tax attorneys, insurers and financial institutions. Having personally sat through my share of insurance sales pitches, I discovered early on that most of these professionals lacked the ability to explain the nature of risk as it pertains to the HSA concept. Agents also struggled to clearly articulate its features, advantages, benefits, and components. Following one such presentation, I asked the agent how long he spent explaining HSAs to prospects.

"It's usually an hour," he replied, "and sometimes, people still don't understand it."

To my mind, the HSA story could be told with a one-page summary and an information graphic for visual learners. Seeing an opportunity, I scheduled a meeting with the agent's sales manager to discuss slashing those 60-minute presentations by half or more. Surprisingly, he was not interested. To him, every minute one of his agents was in front of a prospect was an opportunity to sell something. I can only surmise he was not tracking his team's close rates for HSAs.

The burden the HSA legislation placed on business owners was significant. It required employers to offer HSA-qualified insurance plans as part of their benefit options. Despite a large push inside major corporations, participation rates stayed in the single digits for several years after HSAs were introduced. Employees preferred their traditional employer-managed insurance coverage over the new consumer-selected individual plans. The latter required employees to perform too much of their research. Moreover, the lack of medical pricing information made it difficult for them to compare coverages between the varied high-deductible policies.

Just three years after the launch of HSAs, the vice president of benefits at Aon Consulting at the time, John Reschke, declared, "We should have a lot more people enrolled, but this is a different kind of insurance, and it can be scary at first until people understand." (WSJ, 6/12/2007)[18]

Small business owners without HR departments had to devote considerable time to learning about and explaining the HSA option to their employees. Even more frustrating was the hit owners took to their priorities and the time spent away from everyday management. Despite owners' best efforts, sign-up rates among small businesses remained negligible.

As of 2021, there were approximately 32 million HSAs, about a 10% participation rate.[19] The consensus among critics is that this number has been limited by the high deductible insurance requirement. The cost difference between traditional coverage does not always pencil out for some families, and it puts HSAs completely beyond reach for uninsured Americans and those with non-qualified plans. For individuals who set up their accounts 20 years ago, the program has generated significant savings over time, but the broader objective of leveraging consumers' healthcare choices to rein in healthcare costs overall has not materialized. The lever simply has never gotten big enough.

Policy Impact Is Communications Driven

The Achilles' Heel of HSAs and other promising policy innovations is that all are developed by "policy wonks"—experts who live and breathe within the arcane workings of government for years and years. These professionals amass a depth of knowledge that few other than their peers can grasp in any meaningful way. When one of their initiatives makes it out of the department and into the public sphere, policy wonks assume that the intended beneficiaries will immediately recognize the value and flock to sign up.

Unfortunately, the complicated nature of so many public programs devoted to health insurance, retirement plans, and financial investment renders them impenetrable to the average American. Little if any thought has gone into the potential risk that target constituencies will not sign up, file for, or otherwise take advantage of the programs designed to benefit them. Policy initiatives rolled out with inadequate communications and guidance struggle to achieve the usage rates needed to deliver the intended impact.

At the same time, as soon as high-profile legislation goes into effect, many large corporate entities and interest groups unleash armies of attorneys to find loopholes and workarounds. In many cases, unintended consequences emerge in the months and years following implementation, sending policy wonks, regulators, and legislators back to the drawing board to patch oversights, remove ambiguity, and close loopholes.

Providing Americans greater access to health insurance has been the driving force behind some of the boldest and most innovative legislative initiatives of the 21st Century. All have fallen short of their anticipated goals, however, usually because the benefits and the mechanics of accessing them were not clearly articulated to their intended beneficiaries.

The Affordable Care Act (aka "Obamacare") weighed in at 906 pages when it was introduced for consideration (the comprehensive package was 2700 pages). Upon its passage in 2010, the ACA became famous (or infamous) for getting "yes" votes from members of Congress who only skimmed the bill or relied on summaries provided by their staffers.

The overall thrust of the bill was to reduce the number of uninsured Americans and their families by enrolling them in a wide range of subsidized health insurance plans. A one-stop web portal was intended to be the primary entry point for enrollment, but its development was plagued by problems and delayed for years. At no point during that effort did the roll-out organization anticipate that uninsured Americans, many of whom are poor, were not highly computer literate, nor did they have easy access to computers with reliable Internet service.

The site itself crashed in spectacular fashion when the portal finally opened for business in 2013 (a happenstance that became a case study in IT project train wrecks--but that's for another book). Industry jargon was used widely throughout the portal, leaving it to site visitors to figure out the terminology and sort through the details of the multi-tier plan options.

Plans were categorized into four categories: Bronze, Silver, Gold, and Platinum. These terms were intended to convey increases in cost and quality of coverage, but that hierarchy was never spelled out clearly. Error messages and locked screens were common occurrences daily.

The ACA portal was a website crying out for a product recommendation engine to help mitigate the overwhelming amount of information people needed to process while making their enrollment decisions. Many abandoned the sign-up process altogether after being thoroughly frustrated by the number of choices or by their inability to locate a mechanism that would enable them to compare plans side-by-side.

Ironically, the ACA created an off-shoot industry of consultants and brokers offering to help confused individuals enroll. The health insurance providers also developed a mountain of consumer guides and industry consortium websites like eHealth.com. The confusion caused them to take upon themselves the task of educating the public on how to participate in the ACA benefit. These sites continue to devote considerable digital real estate to explanations about how to qualify for, choose, and enroll in an ACA health insurance policy.

Responsibility for implementing the ACA initiative was delegated to the U.S. Department of Health and Human Services (HHS). The department's goal for enrollment was that seven million previously uninsured individuals and families would obtain policies by the end of the first quarter of 2014. Despite the problems that plagued the website, the total number of initial enrollments reached eight million. History has shown that the program has had a profound impact on uninsured Americans and those locked out of affordable insurance options due to pre-existing health conditions.

As of this writing, almost 16 million Americans have comprehensive health insurance and free preventive care through the Affordable Care Act. However, 30 million remain uninsured. How many of them abandoned the sign-up process because they could not figure out how to enroll? The Cost of Confusion in this example is lost opportunity cost. By failing to get millions more people insured, the healthcare system and taxpayers must bear the higher costs associated with providing care for uninsured patients.

Deregulation: The Confusion of Illusion

For decades, the pendulum of industry regulation has swung slowly back and forth depending on which political party is in the majority at the time. Supporters of free market policies have had significant influence over the last 30 or 40 years in dismantling regulatory frameworks for several industries that impact the daily lives of Americans. The commercial airline industry was among the first high-profile sectors that Congress deregulated in 1978, sending shock waves through the marketplace and hastening the demise of such legendary companies as Pan American Airways,

Transworld Airways (TWA), and other carriers. Despite the economic upheaval, the consensus is that air travel has become much more affordable for the average American family.

For other industries, however, deregulation has been a failure, if not an outright sham. The premise of opening the floodgates to competition has not translated to lower prices. Instead, it has forced consumers to sift through dozens of pitches from unknown providers to resecure the basics of modern life that have had for decades: electricity, natural gas, water, phone service, internet connections, garbage service, and more to come. No legislation has ever considered how to safeguard consumers from being overwhelmed, confused, and, in some cases, victimized by unintended consequences.

Monthly charges for mobile calling plans and fees for cable, satellite and internet service have increased steadily at rates that exceed the average cost-of-living. In Texas, deregulation disconnected the state's entire electric grid from the rest of the company. This exposed customers to the financial risk of periodic peak-time surcharges that tacked hundreds of dollars onto regular monthly bills. Some providers went out of business after only a few years in the market, leaving customers scrambling to sign up with other, higher-priced companies. In February of 2021, an Artic freeze caused statewide outages of not only electricity but also natural gas. At one point, the grid itself was in danger of shutting down, unable to accept electricity from the rest of the country. By the time utilities restarted their generating plants, 246 Texans had died because of the freezing conditions.

Mission Amnesia

All large organizations are what I call "silo-impaired" to one degree or another. Silos occur when teams of employees are grouped and managed according to business functions or professional disciplines rather than working cross-collaboratively. This sets the stage for conflicting goals, misaligned processes, and other inefficiencies, and may spur direct competition and power struggles. A silo-impaired organization always falls short when attempting to deliver a seamless, frictionless flow of value-producing work across departments. When those silos are in government bureaucracies, all these problems become even more entrenched.

Citizens seeking delivery of organizational services that cross the boundaries of multiple silos are almost certain to find the experience frustrating. At the farthest end of the spectrum, the absence of internal clarity can begin to undermine the larger mission of the institutions themselves, negating the premise of good government.

One example on the local level is the building department. Although there is a wide range of opinions about how communities should grow, the primary pressure on housing affordability is a decades-long deficit of residential construction. Had inventory kept pace with demand, median prices across the overall housing market would be substantially lower than they are now. Homeownership would be feasible for many more young families, with all the societal benefits it generates. While there are a variety of factors that builders take into consideration before deciding to break ground, the difficulty of permitting and approval has become an acknowledged disincentive.

Much the same holds true for commercial developers in cities that continue to add onerous requirements. As projects meet with more delays, targets are continually moving, and decision-makers are changing. In Portland, Oregon (the author's home since 1996), global shoe brand Adidas ended up being two years behind schedule on the remodel of a former hospital for its North American headquarters. Among the changing requirements was one that called for the contractor to replace existing healthy trees with smaller trees. The change added months of delays to the project and was compounded by the fact that the types of trees stipulated by the city's tree code could not be found in Oregon. City officials admitted the new tree codes were so complex that its own staff could not figure them out.

Instead of welcoming premier brands and collaborating on successful urban development, the city's building-related bureaus and departments operate within a system that defaults to adversarial relationships. Confusion within and across silos makes the process as difficult as possible.

My wife and I got firsthand experience when we set out to have a new home built while the housing industry was recovering from the 2008 downturn. Things were slow at the county building department because construction had slowed. With costs down for labor and materials locally, we figured it would be a great time to get the most value for our money.

Obtaining the building permit, however, turned out to be a convoluted and maddening. The upfront surveys and plans took a circuitous route across many different desks in the land use office. Reviews and approvals involved geotechnical, environmental, engineering, electrical, plumbing, and other disciplines. If a particular employee happened to be on vacation, things might languish for weeks on that person's desk. The delay in getting the permit issued wreaked havoc on our schedule, pushing construction into the wettest time of the year. We realized we had to become our own "permit expediters," making calls, sending follow-up emails, and showing up in person to check on the status. As a last, I decided to email the director of building services and ask why the process was dragging on so long. After all, during an economic downturn, wouldn't the county want to collect fees and add properties to the tax roll? Fortunately, that broke the logjam. We got a call the next day informing us that our permit was signed and ready to pick up!

Of course, that was just the first chapter of the adventure. By the time the house was completed, we were on a first-name basis with the director and several supervisors. I suggested that each permit application should have a staff person assigned to oversee the flow of pertinent information throughout the organization and keep things on track. I never did hear back about that idea.

Improving the Citizen Customer Experience

What is it like for Americans to interact on an individual basis with the federal government? That is the focus of a major initiative launched in 2022 by The Office of Management and Budget (OMB). An executive order signed by President Joe Biden declared that improving service delivery and customer experience must be fundamental priorities for agencies. The OMB program tasked administrative department with delving into how they operate when dealing with individuals at five major "life intersections" – points at which citizens make life transitions that require a high degree of federal government interaction:

1. Approaching retirement
2. Recovering from natural disaster
3. Moving from active military duty to civilian life
4. Navigating childbirth and early childhood education as a low-income parent
5. Qualifying for critical support due to financial disaster/hardship

These were selected because they involve dealing with multiple agencies and, within those agencies, across a wide range of departmental silos. The starting point for such an effort has to be conducting extensive personal interviews with average Americans who have recently undergone these experiences. This interview will identify key "pain points" that people typically encounter with the various sites, departments, representatives, and administrative tasks (forms, documents, websites, etc.). One objective of the interview will be to obtain information that will enable implementers to develop clear "line-of-sight" process roadmaps so that all stakeholders, providers, and users, have a shared view of the required steps and interactions.

The Biden initiative marks an important shift for the federal bureaucracy, forcing it to become more self-aware of how it impacts individual Americans. It also aims to raise the bar on the quality of the federal government's digital service offerings. As the first foray into customer experience design, this initiative hopes to close the gap between the government's performance and that of the more effective, sophisticated, private-sector service models.

At this juncture, it is anyone's guess whether the initiative will be completed successfully and make recognizable improvements, but points are awarded for the effort.

Adding Confusion to Crisis

Two seismic events have taken place during the writing of this book. The Covid-19 pandemic and the "Stop the Steal" challenge to the integrity of America's election process combined to shake the foundations of American democracy. The question of whether that foundation holds has yet to be answered as both events continue to roil in and out of the news cycle.

Covid-19 Braintrust Fog

One of the first casualties of the pandemic was clear and concise communication. The Centers for Disease Control (CDC) never managed to articulate compelling goals for its Covid-19 response to the public. Much of the fault stems from the failure of policymakers and epidemiologists to agree on a common vocabulary. Vague terms such as *flattening the curve, mitigation, containment,* and *suppression* were used interchangeably. The public confusion that resulted helped undermine the lockdown policies put in place to manage hospital capacity. Instead, hospitals and healthcare professionals were pushed to the brink, overwhelmed by patient counts during the first wave of infections.

Another blind spot was relying on an outdated notion of authority. Historically, the public health functions of government relied on a top-down, parental mode–no doubt a carry-over from the medical profession itself. The doctor always knows best. The CDC's public face was that of an infallible expert with the final word on what the U.S. population should be doing in response to Covid-19. The virus had other plans, however. It became the very definition of a moving target through Its capacity to mutate continually. New strains have increased rates of transmission, produced different symptoms, neutralized prior treatments, and undermined the efficacy of vaccines. With each new wrinkle, the CDC found itself backtracking and changing its guidance, sometimes in direct contradiction of previous decrees. This resulted in ongoing hits to CDC credibility and led to the steady erosion of its power to influence public behavior.

The agency also lost control of the narrative, allowing anti-science, anti-vaccine lobby, and the contrarian intellectuals and pseudo-intellectuals to gain ground. These groups added to the Covid Fog of confusion by weaponizing health information – using real facts to spin false narratives. One tactic was to convert absolute numbers into percentages. It is a trick of perception that minimizes the threat on an individual basis, enabling people to discount the risk. The equation worked like this: focus on the younger age group, count the number of deaths, and divide by the size of the population that is that age. Throughout the pandemic, that result ranged between 1 and 1.5% of all Covid deaths in the U.S. It had the effect of making CDC mask mandates look ridiculous. But for the young people on the wrong side of the equation, 1% is devastating. What's more, is that the health system cannot base is capacity on percentages. It looks at the number of sick people and what it takes to care for them.

Vague Variants

Each new wave of infections introduced an alphabet soup of names and numbers to identify the competing variants of the original virus, SARS-CoV-2. Mutation Delta was followed by Omicron and its ever-evolving progeny, including Alpha, Beta, Gamma and other Greek words appended with alphanumerical designations such as B.1.1.529, BA.2, 3, BQ.1.1, and so on. The naming scheme (or lack thereof), while aiding scientists' communication, remains useless in terms of helping the public assess individual risk levels and make personal choices regarding vaccines, masks, isolation protocols, and other behaviors.

When the World Health Organization announced the most transmissible Omicron variant XBB.1.5 in late 2022, Canadian biology professor Dr. Ryan Gregory began referring to it as "The Kraken," a mythical sea monster, for its ability to overwhelm any immunity acquired through vaccinations or prior infections.[20] Like the Kraken, XBB could destroy everything in its path. The name "went viral" (sorry, I had to do it) and was picked up by the media, leading to an informal worldwide effort to devise "street names" to communicate a meaningful threat level for newly emerging variants. Driving that effort is the shared recognition that the public simply can't be expected to keep the numbers straight when there are 200+ viral variants swirling around the globe.

As history has demonstrated thus far, getting the public to take the virus seriously, maintain vigilance, and adopt preventive behaviors for the long haul was, and will forever be the fundamental challenge. One change the CDC and other public health professionals must adopt is recasting themselves and reframing their profession as one that doesn't always have the answers and set the expectation that the answers are never final because science is always evolving. Answers and recommendations can and should change as more knowledge becomes available.

To prepare for these coming threats, the CDC and other public health professionals must abandon their illusions of infallibility. Better to be "humble experts" who won't always have the answers – and set the expectation that the answers are never final. Health experts' recommendations can and should change as more knowledge becomes available. This will require the agency to undertake a fundamental overhaul of its communication approach and recalibrate its relationship with the American public. As future pandemics emerge, the CDC should rededicate itself to the timeless words of The Hippocratic Oath: "First, do no harm." Leaders must ensure the agency does all it can to prevent confusion, not cause it.

Confusion at The Ballot Box

Citizenship in a democracy comes with certain privileges and corresponding responsibilities. The right to vote goes hand-in-hand with the expectation that voters educate themselves about the issues they will be asked to consider and to seek out reliable information from credible sources. Sadly, that is far from the reality. On average, 45% to 65% of eligible voters participate across major U.S. election cycles. That puts the United States 31st in voter participation rates among 50 countries tracked by the Pew Research Centers.[21]

Given the devastating power of social media to drive wedges between groups and further polarize our society, it is more urgent than ever before to articulate the critical issues that will be decided at the ballot box. Unfortunately, the processes that put issues on the ballot can fall short of that goal, and much of what makes it onto the ballots is driven by money and political advantage.

- *Complex language* that presents ballot measures in technical or legal terminology that is difficult for the average voter to understand and process.
- *Misleading or biased information* can lead to misunderstandings about the implications of a measure, making it seem more favorable or less favorable than it actually will be if implemented.
- *Insufficient Information* prevents voters from being fully informed about the consequences, costs, and other associated factors that would influence whether to pass or reject a ballot measure.
- *Multiple issues on the same ballot* can be overwhelming and confusing to voters, making it difficult for them to fully consider each measure on its own terms and come to an informed decision.

Each of these situations sets the stage for the inadvertent rejection of common-sense ideas, "buyers' remorse" among voters who discover they made the wrong selection on their ballot, or approval of fringe policies that voters did not consider carefully enough.

The independent news site ProPublica featured five of the most confusing ballots in the country in 2012.[22] Florida took top honors with a

12-page ballot covering elected offices and 11 constitutional initiatives drafted by the legislature. Confused Florida voters bombarded citizens' groups like the League of Women Voters with a record number of calls for help with cutting through the jargon.

California Republicans tried to put one over on voters with a proposition worded such that voting "No" actually meant voting "yes" for their new redistricting maps. Voters attempting to preserve the status quo unintentionally triggered an entirely new line-drawing process.

California voters also faced two tax initiatives designed to provide more funding for public schools and early childhood education. Supporters of each measure tried to discredit the other, leaving voters totally confused as they faced near-identical choices.

Each election cycle includes a myriad of ballot measures that generate widespread confusion among voters and widespread displeasure with the outcomes.

Follow the Money

As mentioned, many ballot initiatives are purposefully misleading—taking advantage of voters' lack of knowledge about the real implications of the initiative. Sadly, there is a specialized industry comprised of lobbyists, public relations firms, think tanks and political action committees that are devoted to drafting misleading ballot measures and creating ad campaigns on behalf of special interests.

California's infamous Proposition 13 (1978) was sold to voters as a way to protect their homes from runaway taxes when property values began to increase sharply. The money behind the campaign supporting the measure came from the state's corporate real estate industry, who would reap exponentially more tax benefits than the average homeowner. The result stemmed the growth of the tax base, which became a disaster for schools, local communities and support programs for low-income Californians.

Proposition 13 was packaged with a second, unrelated measure that required a two-thirds vote of both houses of the legislature to raise any revenue at all by new taxation measures—two-thirds votes are nearly impossible to reach. In retrospect, it has become clear that Prop 13 was a misleading fraud that led to decades of public policy strife while providing an economic windfall for corporations.

Special interests have and will continue to pursue their own agendas under the guise of promoting the common good. To counteract this undue influence, voters must become proactive about uncovering hidden details of ballot initiatives. Fortunately, there are nonprofit institutions doing just the same, monitoring developments and using social media to call attention to the reality of measures that are not entirely what they seem.

Government Transformation – All or Nothing

The nationwide civil unrest that took hold across the U.S. as part of the Black Lives Matter movement was especially traumatic for the people of Portland, Oregon. Nightly violence went on for months in 2020, followed by the traumatic impacts of Covid-19 that brought downtown activity to a standstill and fueled the rise in homeless encampments throughout the central city.

Public pressure mounted until city officials set up a commission to review Portland's charter for ways to improve the effectiveness of city government. Portland leaders got more than they bargained for when the Commission referred a ballot measure to voters (Measure 26-228) that would fundamentally alter the nature of the Portland City Council. The measure proposed not one, not two, but three major changes and combined them in an all-or-nothing package.

1. Allowing ranked-choice voting for city council candidates in order of preference, thus eliminating primary elections and nullifying party affiliations.
2. Increasing the size of Portland City Council from 5 to 12 representatives and electing those council members to represent four new geographical districts.
3. Moving from Portland's commission form of government to a professional city manager overseeing all city bureaus.

The city's political establishment joined the business community in lining up against the measure and attempted to have it removed or at least divided into three separate ballot measures. It was not a question of wholesale rejection, as there was widespread agreement that each of the three proposals held promise for addressing the problems. The primary concern was over the enormous scope of the undertaking and the two-year time frame in which it is supposed to be completed. Despite the pushback, the state supreme court upheld the original measure. In November 2022, it was approved by over 58% of Portland voters.

The mayor assembled a task force immediately to begin planning the transition. There is no question that combining all three major changes into one giant transformation effort has upped the stakes substantially—possible even setting it up for failure. Any one of the measures is a "heavy lift" on its own, much less combined. The outlook has been clouded by the exodus of veteran city employees who want no part of what they expect will be a slow-moving train wreck. This loss of institutional knowledge is one of several unintended consequences the commission failed to consider when it decided to bundle all three recommendations into a single up/down vote. More fallout is likely to come before the total Cost of Confusion can be tallied. Portland's motto is "The City that Works." Many voters are wondering whether that will ever be true again.

Confusing Ourselves

Toxic Terminology: How Polarizing Language Prevents the Conversations We Need to Be Having

In his seminal book: "Don't Think of An Elephant," George Lakoff explored the concept of "framing"—the calculated use of language to control the narrative of political issues within the court of public opinion. One of Lakoff's more memorable examples was the term "Death Tax" that Republicans substituted for "estate tax" at every opportunity. Framing the topic with such a stark and emotionally resonant term has enabled the GOP to prevent meaningful examination of estate tax policy to this day.[23]

Framing is among the many tools I have used over the course of a career dedicated to cutting the cost of confusion within global organizations. The terminology and language used to communicate the stakes, technologies, key processes, and other critical information have a profound impact on whether a multi-million-dollar strategic initiative succeeds or fails.

The world's greatest strategic initiative, the American Experiment, stands at a crossroads today due to our failure to recognize that language has just as much power to prevent communication as it does to foster it.

Consider this short list of activist terms that have stoked the culture wars throughout the last election cycle and helped light the fuse for the assault on the United States Capitol on Jan. 6th, 2021: White Privilege, Defund the Police, and Critical Race Theory.

Ostensibly, these terms have risen to prominence owing to the desire of their proponents to bring about genuine societal and political change. Each term is the tip of a huge iceberg of complex issues that need to be surfaced, understood, and compassionately addressed. Unfortunately, each label is doing just the opposite. Rather than serving as a basis for dialogue, these polarizing terms are driving the Left and Right farther and farther apart on the ideological spectrum.

This destructive use of framing has effectively backed almost 50% of the country into a corner. Conservatives and many independent voters feel personally under siege and forced to aggressively defend themselves. The result is no dialogue, no acknowledgement of common ground, and no mutual trust.

So, for progressives who have embraced these galvanizing terms to advocate fiercely for fundamental change, the question is: 'What's my true motivation?" Is it the adrenaline rush of self-righteous indignation and condemnation—or is it a genuine desire to see the country live up to its promises for every race, color, creed, and gender?

On the assumption that it's the latter, I'm going to examine each of the three terms and suggest how choosing different ones might provide a starting point for the critical conversations needed to preserve America's tenuous union.

White Privilege. I must admit, this one pushed my buttons the first time I heard it and never stopped. The problem lies with the word "privilege" and its long-held association with those who are born into wealth and/ or had success handed to them by virtue of their social status and connections. Being told you are privileged feels like a slap in the face to the millions of white middle-class and working-class voters whose bootstrap identity comes from having overcome hardship and earned their way into whatever station of life they find themselves. There are millions of these personal success stories among those now being labeled as the beneficiaries of white privilege. While these Americans may feel humbled and grateful for how their lives have turned out, I think it's fair to say that none of them feels privileged.

That does not mean, however, that this large group of white Americans rejects the underlying idea. Simply changing one word yields a more constructive term with which to reframe the issue for all concerned—*white advantage*. Most white people, including me, can concede that we have had breaks along the way and doors opened to us that would have been slammed in the face of our counterparts of color. White Privilege precludes any conversation. White Advantage makes it possible to start one.

Defund the Police. The tragic murder of George Floyd, a Black man, by white police officers in Minneapolis, Minnesota on May 15, 2022 sent people into the streets nationwide to call attention to the need to drastically rethink the nature of urban policing. The notion of "defunding" law enforcement was, from the outset, an overly simplistic and destructive frame to apply. As someone living just outside downtown Portland, Oregon, I watched as this term not only highjacked an important issue but also literally highjacked the city and served it on a platter to the right-wing pundits and the Republican Party.

As the increasing success of law-and-order candidates has demonstrated, the notion of removing money from police coffers has backfired on the originators of the defunding movement. The rapid increases in crime statistics and murder rates are swinging the pendulum back and closing the window on much-needed reforms. To salvage this opportunity, organizers should consider replacing "defund the police" with *Redefine the Police.*

Getting clarity and consensus around the role of law enforcement with the added dimension of social justice will benefit not only city residents but also the ranks of the police. The latter must be part of the dialogue as equal stakeholders in public safety.

Critical Race Theory. Marking the newest front in the culture wars, this term has come to dominate the news cycle of both right-leaning and left-leaning media outlets. It's also been highjacked by both, as well as by their respective political allies on each side of the proverbial aisle, to stir up more outrage on a daily basis.

Unlike the other two terms under discussion, this one is not a recent addition. It came into use during the late '60s and early '70s to refer to the growing number of critical assessments of the existing legal order from a race-based point of view. Is it a repudiation of all that white Americans hold dear? Absolutely not! Our country needs to own its history—the good and the bad—regarding the treatment and mistreatment of Native Americans and non-white minorities. Unfortunately, the term Critical Race Theory is being used in some states to justify a ban on school curricula designed to expose students to this full picture of American history.

Now that Critical Race Theory has become a toxic term, is there another to replace it? The challenge is to defuse the explosive potency of "race" while keeping it at the center of the examination. Perhaps, an alternative term, such as Built-in Bias or Embedded Discrimination, can cool down the current over-heated rhetoric and create an opening for civil discourse on how systems, structures, and institutions have perpetuated inequality.

Urging activists to abandon toxic terminology is not a request to abandon their principles. It is, however, a request to be honest about their objectives. It's time to choose between language that foments discord and language that fosters dialogue. Replacing the toxic terminology that is stoking our culture wars is an essential first step to repairing the damage we're doing to ourselves. Only through a shared recognition of our country's deepest flaws can we begin to make good on its highest aspirations.

Every country founded on the core principles of democracy requires a collective, ongoing effort to keep citizens informed, educated, and engaged at some basic level. Central to that effort is recognizing that there are lower limits to which the complex socioeconomic issues of our times can be simplified. There are risks at both extremes—overcomplicated and oversimplified—that citizens will withdraw from active participation in the discourse and duties of their self-governing societies. This poses an existential threat to any country built on an intellectual foundation and shared beliefs that must remain vital. Anyone expecting democracy to be a low-effort "no-brainer" should take a hard look at the alternative—authoritarianism.

Even the healthiest of democratic societies now must learn new ways to engage citizens and fight to reclaim mindshare being siphoned off by the Disinformation Economy. This parallel media universe generates huge revenue streams by disseminating inaccurate, biased, and outright falsified information to attract viewers, listeners, subscribers and donors. Purveyors of disinformation are able to reap tremendous financial rewards while hiding behind First Amendment protections of free speech. How to combat the toxic influence of the Disinformation Economy may be the most important debate of the modern age.

Chapter 5

Confusion As A Strategy

The bulk of this book is devoted to exploring the unintentional and unrecognized impacts of confusion. It is equally—if not more important—to understand that confusion can be sown willfully and used strategically by organizations, business sectors, and assorted "bad actors" across the geopolitical landscape.

In the case of the latter, targeted misinformation campaigns are implemented continually to disrupt elections, destabilize countries, and foment political and cultural polarization. Russia, China, and North Korea are the most widely recognized practitioners of the dark art of social media manipulation. Many books have already been written about the ease with which these regimes exploit technology platforms and subvert the idealism of those who created them.

To counter these threats, dedicated cybersecurity teams around the world monitor misinformation and work with global technology platforms to remove the worst offending campaigns. Mainstream media outlets are the next layer of defense. The rest of the responsibility lies with us to manage our exposure and attempt to educate others in our personal orbits. The latter has become a Herculean task that will continue for as long as we participate in social media networks.

The Gorgon's Knot of Legalese

The practice of "fostering confusion" is not something that arrived with the advent of the Internet. It has been in use for decades in certain professions and business sectors. Two examples familiar to most people are unscrupulous lawyers and insurance companies.

Even well-intentioned legal documents, contractual agreements, and judicial rulings are notorious for their length, density, and incomprehensibility by all but other attorneys. Referred to as "legalese," the formal and technical language reserved for legal documents has interesting roots. A short detour into cultural anthropology helps to explain.

DOI: 10.4324/9781003301080-5

There is the oft-told story that modern legal tradition's problems began in Elizabethan England when a significant percentage of the population did not read or write. When documents were needed for any legal or business purpose, the illiterate citizenry relied on the services of lawyers,solicitors, and scriveners. In the era before retainers and hourly fees, these professionals were *charged by the word* for their services! Consequently, attorneys had a direct financial incentive to make documents as long and convoluted as possible. Unable to read the documents they commissioned, clients were none the wiser. Over time, the situation set the stage for cultural and professional acceptance of unnecessary wordiness and elaboration.

Today, however, the problem of dense and seemly incomprehensible legalese stems more from the lawyers' attempt to be proactive. Legal documents have grown longer and denser through attorneys' efforts to anticipate future problems and prevent their occurrence by addressing them in advance. The profession is further constrained by having to incorporate words and phrases that have a different meaning in the legal context than they have in the common, everyday context. Much of this confusion is mandated by the fact that failure to comply with these legalese requirements creates a fertile ground for malpractice lawsuits. These confusing legal definitions and usages are created in case law, legislation, and regulations, much of which are inaccessible to the ordinary person.

As a close relative of the legal profession, the insurance business has a vested interest in sowing confusion among the policyholders and service providers the industry purports to serve. The premium-based business model is scaled such that large volumes of regular payments accrue to create a multi-million-dollar investment vehicle. Mission statements to the contrary, the primary job of an insurance company is making money with the big pile of money its policyholders send in each month. Paying claims is secondary. Consequently, insurance companies want to hold onto every dollar as long as they can. The industry relies on overwhelming amounts of "fine print"—indecipherable policy language to confuse purchasers and innumerate vast numbers of "exclusions" to coverage, liability, and payouts.

As a business with very strong ties with the legal profession, the insurance industry is a heavy user of legalese. This is because most of its documents are drafted within the legal context, as are almost all legally binding documents in the commercial world.

Unfortunately, the legal and proactive nature of these documents necessarily creates confusion in the mind of the ordinary consumer. Well-meaning insurers have begun to address this problem through consumer outreach. Websites feature Frequency Asked Questions (FAQs) to explain key points to the average layman. Overall, simplifying the language of plans and coverage is a major thrust of the industry.

The confusing legalese situation, however, can be easily exploited when bad intent is involved in the drafting of a document. An unscrupulous insurance company, for example, has a vested interest in sowing confusion among the policyholders and service providers it purports to serve. The premium-based business model is scaled to generate large volumes of regular payments that can be accrued to create a multi-million-dollar investment vehicle out of monies in excess of what is spent servicing customers.

Mission statements to the contrary, the primary job of an insurance company beyond paying claims is to accrue a large reserve from the cash flow of premiums paid by policyholders each month. The reserve has two purposes: first, to meet future high, extraordinary, and unexpected claims (think tornados and covid), and second, to be invested and earn returns that both increase the reserves and make money for the stockholders. Consequently, there is a strong incentive for insurance companies to hold onto every dollar for as long as they can.

The industry generates overwhelming amounts of "fine print"—indecipherable policy language that confuses purchasers and enumerates vast numbers of "exclusions" affecting coverage, liability, and payouts. Also in the fine print are numerous and varied exclusions (e.g., acts of God) and exceptions (i.e., no coverage in certain situations). An unscrupulous insurance company will bury or finesse these barriers to claims in convoluted or obscure paragraphs and not provide any FAQ information that might alert the policyholder to them. This behavior often results in shock, anger, and dismay when policyholders are informed their losses are only partially covered or, worse, not covered at all.

Navigating the Health Insurance Maze

Some insurance company processes are so convoluted or restrictive that health providers refuse to accept the company on their roster of allowable insurance. Other insurance providers are welcome.

Even when well-intentioned, claim processes can be convoluted. Some less benign companies seem to have designed their process to move slowly so that the company can hold onto premiums for as long as legally permitted. This tactic both maximizes interest income and discourages claims.

Unfortunately, no organization does that better than medical insurers—organizations that are controlling what is arguably the most stressful aspect of every day—health. Some of these companies are notorious for dragging out or unfairly restricting payments to the myriad of healthcare entities involved in hospital stays—payouts to the facilities, attending physicians, radiologists, laboratory technicians, surgeons, pharmacies, physical therapists, and more. The aging reports of these providers' receivables from some insurance companies are enough to give accountants heart attacks!

As an aside, I note that this hold-onto-reserves game has also surfaced in the property and casualty market. Some providers in this market are now challenging this practice this historical practice in an effort to differentiate themselves from competitors. Their rejection of it is based on the idea that fast settlements make policyholders happy. They also believe that a fast response can be more economical in the long run when compared to long, drawn-out claims processing. These remain exceptions to the rule to pay claims as late as possible.

An even more efficient way to hold onto the money is to reduce direct payments in favor of reimbursement. This shifts the upfront cost for covered expenses to policyholders/providers. The patient must pay their provider directly for services, tests, and drugs and then file claims with the insurance company to receive money back for all covered expenses. Other times, the provider assumes the cost upfront and then spends countless hours repeatedly requesting reimbursement. The more burdensome the submission process (e.g., multiple forms to fill out, copies of all receipts, explanations from providers, mail-in versus online, etc.), the more likely people will be discouraged from filing their claims in the first place. To extend the delay, this type of rapacious company will circle back with additional information requests before it approves a claim and issues a check. To add insult to injury, a slow, piecemeal payment system often means that patients continue to receive bills months after their medical discharge.

Many families face sticker shock for outstanding balances resulting from coverage limits, exclusions, and complicated formulas for meeting deductibles and out-of-pocket maximums. Skyrocketing medical costs combined with this cost of confusion surcharge are devastating across low- and middle-income families as well as fixed-income seniors.

The federal government, often through the auspices of Medicare, has implemented regulations to make insurance policies more understandable for the average consumer. Unfortunately, the opposite has also been true. Frequently extreme confusion has stemmed from the government's communications about its efforts to "do good." This is most evident from the complexity it has created in the insurance ecosystem: think… wait for it… *more* insurance options!

The beleaguered health insurance consumer is now confronted with choices involving Medi-Gap plans, Health Savings Accounts, the ACA (Obama Care), tiered Advantage and Supplemental plans, and other offerings. The intent is good. It's an effort to protect insured healthcare consumers from huge, unexpected medical bills. The result is confusion.

Ironically, the numerous policy solutions fall short of delivering their benefits because the selection and use of the programs are frequently as convoluted and confusing for individuals to navigate as the insurance industry itself. This situation explains why the number of Americans leaning toward supporting the universal health care approach (aka Medicare for All) has steadily risen from 37% in 2002 to a high of 63% in 2020. (Pew Research Centers)[24]

In the meantime, so long as their processes and writings remain impenetrable and complex, whether as a matter of practice or intentionally, the US's massive insurance conglomerates will remain among the most profitable organizations on the planet.

When "Free" is Just a Four-letter Word

Savvy marketers recognize the power of high-visibility promotional tools to boost sales and build brand awareness. Giveaways, sweepstakes, bonus items, and product rebates are among the traditional tactics used to create visibility and influence purchase decisions. Seeing a product that includes a rebate, most shoppers instinctively "do the math" and subtract the rebate amount from the selling price of the item. In many cases, that quick calculation becomes the deciding factor in choosing which product to purchase. Actually, getting that money in hand is a different story.

According to Consumer World founder Edgar Dworsky, between 40% and 60% of rebates are never redeemed (consumerworld.org). Other advocates have estimated that $500 Million in manufacturers' rebates go unclaimed each year. Companies make redemption as difficult and burdensome as possible for customers by using a variety of tactics to complicate the process. Short time windows for filing, special forms, mail-in-only submission, multiple hard-copy receipts for proof of purchase, and more hair-splitting conditions cause many to abandon the process midstream. For those who complete their claims, failure to meet detailed requirements in the letter provides grounds for high rejection rates. For rebates that are accepted and paid, issuing debit cards instead of mailing checks is another tactic that reduces the number and total amount of payouts.

Debate the rebate! Before discounting the list price in their heads, buyers who find themselves drawn to the item with a rebate offer should consider the likelihood of ever putting that money back into their wallets.

Keeping the Fair Out of Airfare

Since the U.S. Congress passed the Airline Deregulation Act of 1978, the median cost of a round-trip airline ticket has declined, making travel more accessible to millions of people around the world. The downside is that deregulation unleashed the airlines' ability to create multiple additional revenue streams by systematically unbundling (and often eliminating) services that, historically, had been included in the ticket price. Things that used to be "free"—checked luggage, in-flight food and beverage service, seat assignments, overhead storage, carry-on bags, flight changes, and more—are now charged separately and generating huge amounts of bottom-line revenue.

According to the U.S. Department of Transportation (DOT), airlines collected $5.3 Billion in baggage fees in 2021. Change and cancellation fees exceeded $700 Million. The list of extras for which flyers now must fork over additional fees includes legroom, priority boarding, and in-flight Internet.

Moreover, many of the industry's fee practices are deliberate attempts to seed confusion and prevent comparison shopping by consumers. Some carriers cloak fee policies in complexity and often hide them until the last page of the online purchase process. A new practice among discount airlines is waiting to disclose baggage and seat selection fees until passengers check in at the airport. The choice is to pay up or go home. Oh, and that reaction will incur a cancellation fee, by the way!

The battle for pricing transparency in the airline industry has been ongoing since 2014, when the DOT proposed new rules for disclosing checked bag fees and advance seating upcharges during the online booking process. However, the industry has used lawsuits to stop that effort and has continued to resist and prevent meaningful protections for consumers. The DOT began another push in 2020 in response to the introduction of new "no-frills" fare designations that come with a range of limitations, exclusions, and other fine print policies. According to the department, there is still too much traveler confusion. Whether the stricter disclosure rules come to pass remains to be seen. In the meantime, booking air travel requires paying closer attention than ever—before you hit the "Purchase Now" button!

Into the Labyrinth of Healthcare Costs

Just a bit more on the US healthcare situation. Competition is one of the silver bullets most touted by policymakers to fight the rising cost of healthcare. The argument goes that giving pricing information to consumers will empower them to shop around and make more informed choices on where to spend their healthcare dollars. According to the theory, this will put pressure on providers across the board to lower their costs for routine tests, procedures, and surgeries.

At the start of 2021, the Centers for Medicare and Medicaid Services (CMS) policy for hospital price transparency went into effect. These federal guidelines require hospitals to provide "...clear, accessible pricing information online." According to the CMS website, "This information will make it easier for consumers to shop and compare prices across hospitals and estimate the cost of care before going to the hospital." (CMS.org)[25]

The policy looks great on paper, but like all such policy attempts to give consumers a break, this one is fraught with loopholes and exceptions. The fundamental flaw, however, is the assumption that healthcare is a DIRECT PURCHASE. That is simply not the case.

The reality is that 92% of the US population has some form of health insurance (average 2021 estimates). (Census.gov)[26] Rarely does someone pay the full cost out of pocket, so the idea of patient price shopping is a bit of an illusion regarding the power of individuals and families to "take charge" of medical expenses. It is the insurance industry that wields the bulk of control through tens of thousands of negotiated price agreements on everything from the charges for physicians, lab tests, and routine procedures to room rates for out-patient, in-hospital, and intensive care.

Still, price transparency has left a few skeletons out of the closet in the cases where consumers have uncovered multiple prices for a procedure *in the same hospital.* Others have found that prices can vary across a multi-site hospital system, depending on which facility a patient chooses.

While the CMS rules on price transparency have created the illusion that competitive forces will lower costs for consumers, the curtain remains tightly shut when it comes to figuring out in advance what that trip to the hospital will cost someone WITH insurance that has a deductible. Try getting that answer from an insurance company or a doctor prior to checking in for treatment!

No one is afforded visibility ACROSS all the various cost centers, so any estimate comes with a list of caveats and disclaimers. It is only weeks later, when the statements come pouring in, that the amounts shown under "PATIENT'S RESPONSIBILITY" can be added up to reveal the actual out-of-pocket cost. This is beginning to change through requirements that out-of-network providers must notify patients and obtain written consent prior to providing care.

Thus far, hospital price transparency is the policy equivalent of shuffling deck chairs on the Titanic. It doesn't change the fact that we are still going to drown in the ever-rising cost of healthcare. In lieu of universal health care, what's needed is an incentive for the insurance companies to advocate for their policyholders to get both the best healthcare and the best value healthcare. Giving all Americans access to Medicare's negotiated rates would be a great first step. Another mechanism might offer tax advantages or rebates based on the accuracy of pre-admission estimates against the actual out-of-pocket payments. The closer those two numbers are, the better for consumers trying to prepare financially for in-hospital treatment and follow-up care.

Facing the challenges of creating a high-quality and equitable healthcare system demands clarity, not confusion.

Confusion is for SAPs

Nothing is more disruptive to a corporate workforce than undergoing the transition to a new business management software system. These technology platforms require organizations to completely "rewire" legacy workflows and ditch individual accounting and management applications in favor of a massive, integrated system. The most ubiquitous of these platforms is one called Systems Applications and Systems in Data Processing or SAP.

SAP implementation is so complex that it requires the use of third-party companies known as "integrators." These firms understand the nuances of SAP core systems and the add-on modules that provide specialized functionality. Integrator teams interface with client user groups to understand their business requirements, determine the appropriate SAP functions and features needed, and then use this information to direct programmers to tailor the underlying software accordingly.

It's a lucrative business that has attracted the world's largest consulting firms. Many have figured out ways to make it even more lucrative by leveraging confusion across their client's organizations. Here's how that works. The sales team pitches the promise of a fast-track implementation to the board of directors and senior leadership team. This helps to offset any concerns about a lengthy disruption that could reduce productivity and cause a potential hit to operational performance/revenue. Given that SAP initiatives typically run into seven figures, anything that at least minimizes the disruptive impact sounds good to executive decision-makers.

As soon as the ink is dry on the contract, the consultants swarm across the organization to meet with employees on a department-by-department basis. The interactions are intended to introduce client users to SAP capabilities. In these interactions, consultants try to understand the role of each department and how it currently operates within the enterprise. The focus is on capturing the types and sources of business information each group works with: the inputs/outputs to and from that department, and any other workflow considerations specific to that department. In sum, the upfront information-gathering effort is used to establish the requirements and functional specifications that will be used to tailor SAP's sprawling platform to the needs of the specific client.

The consultants return to their hive, where programmers begin to tailor and tune the SAP capabilities to accommodate the client organization's needs. Functional rollouts begin with detailed orientation and training sessions for employees. The integrator keeps the pedal to the metal so it can meet the aggressive schedule and win the incentivized payment milestones.

The outcome? The SAP system gets installed on time and on target—what's not to like?

Fast forward several months to experience the dark underbelly of fast-track SAP integration. As employees gain a better understanding of working with and within the global application, they begin to discover critical business functions that are missing, data points that are not being captured, and processes that are out of alignment with other parts of the organization. More tech-savvy users feel the frustration and see the unrealized potential that was left on the table in the rush to get the SAP up and running

Don't Let the Price Fool You—Understanding the Cost of Acquisition

A common theme to several of the examples in this chapter is the advantage of keeping people confused about how much they ultimately will spend to achieve their goals, whether it be for a flight, a medical procedure, or a global software package. The concept at work here is the distinction between the *purchase price* and the *cost of acquisition*. The former—price—typically is just one component of the latter. The price is the specified amount needed to buy an item or a service; however, there may be other costs involved in taking possession of an item and getting full use of it. Those costs are also components of the cost of acquisition. For example, taking a trip involves making an airline reservation, involves the price of the ticket PLUS taxes and fees. Then, there are seat upgrades and baggage fees to consider, transportation to/from the airport, long-term parking, and more. The sum of the purchase price plus all the additional amounts is the total cost of acquisition of that trip—and that total cost should be a factor in every purchasing decision. Comparing purchase prices alone does not ensure that you are getting the highest value for your money. Make sure to review the fine print for extras, add-ons, and other costs over and above the agreed-upon price.

quickly. In both cases, the integrator consultant gets to come back and charge for a whole new scope of work while racking up billable hours.

The foundation for these ongoing back-end revenue streams, whether intentional or not, gets set at the front end of engagements. By rushing through the needs and requirements phase at the outset, integrators prevent employees from developing a meaningful grasp of what SAP does and what it could do for their departments. It fails to adequately capture their knowledge and creativity. Consequently, initiatives managed like this are bound to leave people feeling overwhelmed and confused and disrespected. This experience also engenders significant resistance to the changes required to use the SAP or prevents them from using the sophisticated software in ways that deliver its full value to the workplace.

For readers who find themselves considering a technology-driven change in their organizations, pay close attention if vendors promise a quick and easy implementation. Sound the alarm and put the brakes on by asking lots of questions and encouraging peers to do the same. An organization that takes time to understand fully what it's getting itself into will see a much higher return on its investment (ROI), derive more operational benefit over the lifecycle of the technology, and have happier user-employees.

Confusion in the Courtroom

When it comes to the calculated application of confusion, the legal profession sets the bar. Civil suits are especially fertile territory for complicated arguments backed by tsunamis of information. As attorneys research and build their case strategy, they typically go deep into the weeds to pull out every relevant fact, a shred of supporting evidence, and expert witness. It is only natural to want judges and jurors to have the same deep level of knowledge to ensure the desired verdict. [not really] The decider at trial can get lost in the minutiae and fail to discern the main strands of the most effective arguments. Too much information can clutter the roadmap leading to a correct decision. This happens when the imparted facts do not buttress the potentially winning arguments. Litigators try hard to identify the winning themes and then use only the information that supports those themes and discard those that are minimally or unhelpful.

At the other end of the strategic spectrum, a legal team can choose to use cluttering but frequently emotionally charged irrelevant information to achieve its desired outcome. When advocating for a losing case, some trial lawyers will try to present irrelevant information and witnesses for the sole purpose of dumping distracting, manipulative, and emotionally-charged information into the trial. Of course, the opposing attorney's role and the judge's countering role in this situation is to object and to sustain the objection, thereby keeping the information out. The incentive for the judge is to avoid the trial outcome from being overturned on appeal because irrelevant, prejudicial information was allowed in. Judges hate being overturned on appeal because it directly reflects on their skills. They know that such less-than-ethical tactics can yield a valid appeal or mistrial.

Defendants will assert that the confusion approach has been used increasingly by attorneys leading class action lawsuits against manufacturers of a wide range of consumer products. Cases involving securities and investment fraud are another area in which the complexities of accounting, financial reporting, and other arcane subjects can be difficult for citizen jurors to grasp and render decisions confidently. Of course, litigators on the other side point to the same tactics being used by the overwhelming numbers of opposing attorneys they face at trial. Only through jurors' (and judges') diligent efforts to make sense of the arguments does justice prevail.

The Smartest Crooks in The Room

Speaking of energy, if this chapter on weaponized confusion were to have one organizational poster child, it would have to be Enron. More than 20 years after it imploded, the company still holds the record for the longest corporate con game of the 21st Century.

The lingering compound question is: "How did they get away with it, and for so long?"

A common thread through the investigations and legal proceedings was a company culture that celebrated complexity and maintained a certain "black box mystique." The unspoken assertion was, "You wouldn't understand it even if we explained it to you."

Enron's cultivated arrogance permeated the C-suite, as evidenced by a series of complex equations written on the whiteboard of the conference room adjacent to CFO Andrew Fastow's office. When asked if he understood them, Fastow replied, "I pulled them out of a book to intimidate people." (WSJ, 8/26/02)

There also was a conscious effort to keep people "in the dark" both inside and outside of the organization.

"They didn't explain things," said analyst Jim McAuliffe of Morgan Stanley Dean Witter. "They were very cocky and self-assured." (Corpwatch. org.)[28] com)

As losses from risky bets began piling up, the company went to great lengths to make its filings as obscure as possible. Consider this excerpt from the 2001 second quarter report: *Enron entered into share settled costless collar arrangements... The transactions resulted in noncash increases in assets and equity.*[29]

Say what??? Financial analysts simply could not decipher this stuff, nor could employees and retirees whose life savings had been poured into Enron stock.

The problem with weaponizing confusion is that it is unsustainable. Eventually, some people wise up—and you get caught. In the end, it was left to the Securities and Exchange Commission and congressional committees to pull back the curtain on Enron's murky deals, conflicts of interest, executive improprieties, and failures of corporate governance.

Digital Dollars—Enter at Your Own Risk

Beyond its initial repercussions, the Enron debacle was a wake-up call for the need to overhaul financial regulation, close loopholes, and standardize accounting methods to foster greater transparency across all publicly traded companies. In some ways, Enron's "black box" became a Pandora's Box, unleashing the first generation of complex, high-risk investment vehicles: derivatives, tranches, interest rate swaps, and more.

Today, this segment of the investment world is beyond the realm of understanding for any but the most well-trained and knowledgeable professionals. The career investors and financial institutions that operate in this rarified market have the know-how to leverage its complexity to maintain its exclusivity. Even so-called "One-Percenters" (the uber-wealthy) understand the advantages they have enjoyed from the use of confusion as a strategy in the investment world.

In the two-plus decades since Enron's demise, financial markets have been flooded with ever more exotic trading vehicles. Indecipherable jargon and acronyms are rampant, especially among blockchain promoters and cryptocurrency platforms. Terms such as tokenized assets, NFT (non-fungible token), crypto wallets, and gamification marketing are light years beyond the general public's understanding of investment. This factor is also the reason that so-called "meme stocks" have lured hordes of inexperienced investors into the market. A new wave of digital investor communities and E-trading websites have blurred the lines between prudent investment and online casinos.

Bitcoin and other blockchain based currencies have upended traditional banking but have also been subject to huge swings in value. Several of these players have been robbed of hundreds of millions of dollars in a matter of minutes courtesy of international hackers. Since "peak crypto" in November 2020, the combined losses across all cryptocurrencies through January 2023 have exceeded $2 Trillion! The bricks-and-mortar economy has survived because the bulk of those losses were reflected in the digital accounts of institutional investors and savvy traders. Many people, however, lost their life savings, including retirees who went all in, encouraged by the media hype.

In this digital Wild West, investors face greater and more widespread risk than many of them fail to fully grasp, nor are they prepared for the scope of losses they have experienced. As of this writing, customers of crypto market maker FTX have lost $8 billion in deposits due to fraudulent loans and asset transfers to the company's founders. The potential for recovery of the funds is slim to none.

The federal government's Securities and Exchange Commission and congressional leaders are looking actively into bringing more oversight and regulation to the cryptocurrency markets. How soon that produces meaningful protection for investors is anybody's guess. Perhaps, the best advice is this time-tested reminder: "Never invest in something you don't understand." Toward that end, increasing the public's level of financial literacy—and our own—is the best counterstrategy for protecting investors.

Calculated efforts to create confusion show no signs of stopping or being regulated effectively. The least of them cost us money and time. The largest efforts do irreparable harm, weaponizing confusion in an assault upon civil discourse and democratic societies around the globe. Maintaining vigilance is our best defense. Our best offense is insisting on clarity and transparency. Bottom line: where there are smoke and mirrors, there is bound to be a Cost of Confusion.

Chapter 6

Deadly Confusion

The previous chapters of this book addressed the somewhat abstract exercise of calculating the Cost of Confusion in dollars and hours. This chapter explores the facets of confusion whose cost is measured in human lives: accidents, disasters, tragedies, terrorist attacks, and the responses to them.

How Confusion Spirals Out of Control

First, full discloser and a disclaimer: no neurobiologists or other qualified scientists were consulted for this topic. Their level of expertise is not required to recognize that confusion is a dynamic state of mind. This affects not only cognitive functions but also behavior, both conscious and unconscious. A myriad of factors determines how we experience confusion at any given moment—whether we feel more confused or less as our brains receive additional information and sensory input. Sight, sound, touch, smell, or taste can provide data that contribute to thought processes and response behavior.

To understand how and why confusion can lead to deadly consequences, consider confusion in the context of a continuum or escalating set of experiences. In Figure 6.1, confusion anchors the left side. To the right are three primary emotional states that confusion can morph into as an individual is subjected to increasing amounts of stress and environmental stimuli.

As a person moves through each state, cognitive capacity declines, and behavior becomes more volatile. This is a result of the human body's "flight or fight" response involving the release of primary stress hormones adrenaline and cortisol. The amounts of these hormones and the speed with which they are released are affected by external stressors and environmental stimuli. The interaction of all these factors determines how quickly an individual will progress through this continuum.

DOI: 10.4324/9781003301080-6

HOW CONFUSION ESCALATES

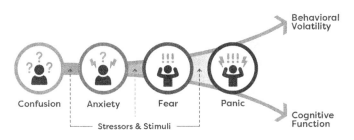

Figure 6.1

Here is a scenario to help unpack the concept.

A driver confused by detour signs ends up on the streets of an unfamiliar neighborhood. After a few minutes, the driver starts to worry and feels anxious and agitated about being lost. Suddenly, there is a gunshot! Immediately, that confused, anxious driver ramps to full panic mode. Without thinking or looking, the driver accelerates, runs a red light, and strikes a pedestrian. Confusion has turned deadly in a matter of seconds.

Stressors can come from anywhere. They could be deadlines, financial worries, a lack of sleep, or too many distractions. Stressors may also include a range of other emotions that trigger stress hormones, for example, irritation, embarrassment, or anger. They can become a torrent that spirals out of control into violent physical altercations. This mix is especially deadly when a firearm is within easy reach. Confusion is a very real catalyst for the impulsive behavior linked regularly to random gun violence.

Along with stressors, environmental stimuli are contributing factors to confusion with deadly consequences. The sight of blood, the smell of smoke, the sound of breaking glass, a hot blast of air, a taste of pepper spray—any of these can drive people across the continuum of confusion.

Experts in crowd control know too well how swiftly mass chaos can arise when crowds in confined spaces are startled by a loud noise or people headed to the stadium exits feel the pressure of jostling bodies building behind them.

Understanding the ways in which confusion escalates and the circumstances that contribute to it are key to protecting ourselves and others.

Pay Attention: This Is a Drill

Safety experts, first responders, and the military no doubt have a far better understanding of how confusion turns deadly. There are decades of research into human behavior under duress and in response to accidents, fires, natural disasters, and major casualty events. These are situations in which individuals' judgment is impaired, and they may be incapable of calm, rational behavior.

There is reasoning behind drills. Fire drills, earthquake drills, evacuation drills, and more are used to prepare individuals and organizations to respond effectively in emergency situations. The core objective of a drill is to engrain behaviors, protocols, procedures, and routes so that people can follow them almost without thinking. This makes drills an important counterbalance to the risks posed by the confusion that spirals out of control.

The purpose of fire drills is to familiarize individuals with the evacuation route and procedures, to identify any obstacles that may slow down the evacuation process, and to train individuals to evacuate quickly and calmly.

Drills prepare individuals for a wide range of emergencies, such as earthquakes, hurricanes, or active shooter situations. Participants practice activating emergency plans, communicating with emergency responders, and following emergency procedures.

The effectiveness of drills depends just as much, if not more, on ensuring the same high level of clear, concise information organizations use to manage workflow or sell products. If drills become an afterthought, there is a greater risk of injuries and fatalities in the event of an actual emergency. There is no margin of error that allows for confusing instructions or missing signage. Preventing the Cost of Confusion is not a drill.

Disastrous Response

Some of the research for this book involved wading through the many analyses written in the wake of modern American disasters. It was not hard to spot evidence of confusion and consider the roles it played before, during, and after these events. This section briefly explores three examples: the terrorist attacks on September 11, 2001, Hurricane Katrina in late August 2005, and the mass shooting at Robb Elementary in Uvalde, Texas, on May 24, 2022. All are examples of the near impossibility of preparing for the unimaginable. The Uvalde tragedy may forever defy understanding.

9/11

Terrorists weaponized two commercial airliners to destroy the twin towers of the World Trade Center. The attacks resulted in such unfathomable levels of death, destruction, and chaos that the concept of emergency response was pushed into uncharted territory. Along with physical dangers, there were enormous challenges adding to the confusion that overtook the city in the moments after the first plane struck the North Tower.

One of the main sources of confusion in the emergency response was the lack of information about the extent of the damage and the number of casualties. With limited access to the World Trade Center site, law enforcement and fire department crews had no way to determine how many people were trapped, where they were located, or how fires and structural damage would impact rescue.

One of the most crippling aspects was the inability of fire and rescue teams (NYFD) to communicate directly with their police counterparts (NYPD). Emergency communication systems initially were disrupted by the widespread damage, but there was a more shocking reason for the literal disconnect. Firefighters and police officers at the World Trade Center site had difficulty communicating with each other, as well as with other agencies, due to the different radio frequencies and systems they used. Because radios were incompatible, they could not be used for joint coordination at the site. This inability to share intelligence about conditions at Ground Zero is thought to have contributed significantly that day to the number of casualties not only among civilians but also first responders.

Another factor was the unclear lines of authority and the effect that lack of clarity had on decision-making processes. From the outset, there was confusion at the New York City Emergency Command Center about who was in charge. Ultimately, the emergency response expanded to encompass multiple state and federal agencies. Throughout the day and during the aftermath, these agencies had conflicting priorities, misunderstandings, and disagreements over how to manage the response, all of which slowed down rescue efforts and compromised effectiveness.

Miscommunication on 9/11 was not limited to NYC. The Federal Aviation Administration (FAA) failed to immediately notify NORAD of the hijackings, leading to a significant delay in the military intervention that might have prevented the additional attack on the Pentagon. Additionally, there was uncertainty over who had the authority to scramble fighter jets. This further delayed the military response. When the FAA issued the order to stop air traffic and ground all flights, there was genuine concern that civilian planes could be shot down accidentally due to the "fog of war." Fortunately, this did not happen. Planes remained grounded for two days before airlines could begin the enormous coordination effort of safely getting flights back in the air and passengers to their final destinations. Air travel would never be the same.

In the years following the attacks, congressional hearings and investigations analyzed the response effort, issued findings, and made recommendations. These have since to make their way into wide-ranging policies and procedures that acknowledge the deadly impact of confusion had on the emergency response. The lessons learned—ensuring there are clear lines of authority, effective communication systems, and accurate and up-to-date information—have helped to improve emergency preparedness and response procedures in the years since the attacks.

Hurricane Katrina

Despite the lessons learned from 9/11, the emergency response to Hurricane Katrina in 2005 was compromised by some of the same types of confusion. When the hurricane made a direct hit on New Orleans beginning on August 29, the region faced many of the same challenges.

Like 9/11, the disaster response involved multiple federal, state, and local agencies, each with its own jurisdiction and responsibilities. The various responders had difficulty agreeing on which group was in charge, setting priorities, assigning specific actions, and coordinating joint efforts for more effective response.

Katrina, of course, was a very different disaster from 9/11. Flood waters devastated historic neighborhoods; slow rescue efforts resulted in many residents being trapped inside their homes, where they were drowned by rising water. As was the case during 9/11 in New York, communication breakdowns contributed to confusion in the early hours of the disaster. Emergency responders had difficulty communicating with each other and with command centers, which led to misunderstandings and delayed response times. This resulted in confusion about the status of rescuers, the location of missing individuals, and where additional resources needed to be dispatched.

Those residents who managed to escape gathered in downtown New Orleans where the city's sports arena, the Superdome, became the shelter of last resort. The initial plan was using the arena as a temporary shelter for residents displaced by the storm. However, the facility and its staff quickly became overwhelmed by the sheer number of people seeking refuge, as well as the limited resources available to care for them. The lack of adequate supplies, such as food, water, and medical care, and the unsanitary conditions led to chaos and desperation among the survivors. The absence of effective evacuation plans, as well as the slow response from government agencies, left people with no place else to go.

The situation at the Superdome became a symbol of the larger failures in the response to Hurricane Katrina. It highlighted the lack of preparedness, the poor coordination between government agencies, and the slow and inadequate response to the crisis. Much of the blame has been assigned to the Federal Emergency Management Agency (FEMA). The agency showed all the signs of an organization that lacked understanding of the situation and was confused about how to respond to the disaster. This confusion ultimately contributed to the high number of lives lost and the huge scale of the suffering.

Despite warnings of a potential disaster, FEMA was not fully prepared to respond to the scale of the destruction caused by the hurricane and widespread flooding that left residents homeless. FEMA arrived with insufficient resources, equipment, and personnel. Consequently, the agency's response was slow and disorganized, which only exacerbated the situation. The agency was criticized for its slow distribution of supplies, poor communication with local officials, and inadequate evacuation plans. In the end, it was simply not up to the important task of coordinating the relief efforts among state and local governments, non-profit organizations, and the military.

Although the National Hurricane Center has adjusted Katrina's death toll downward to 1,392, from an earlier estimated 1,833 deaths, it [Hurricane Katrina] still accounts for the second-highest U.S. death toll for weather disasters in modern times.)[30]

In fairness, natural disasters will never be managed to everyone's satisfaction, especially those directly impacted. Fortunately, Hurricane Katrina became a major turning point for FEMA and served as a wake-up call. In the years since Katrina, the agency has taken steps to clarify its mission and improve its preparedness and response capabilities. It remains a work in progress.

Uvalde School Shooting

On the morning of May 24, 2022, a troubled 18-year-old teenager entered an unlocked side door of Robb Elementary in Uvalde, Texas. Wielding an automatic rifle he had purchased the day before, the gunman barricaded himself in a fourth-grade classroom and methodically began to shoot students and teachers trapped there and in an adjoining room. The death toll was 19 students and two teachers. The first shots were reported at approximately 11:36am local time. When police finally stormed the room and killed the gunman, the time was 12:50pm.

It was the deadliest school shooting in Texas history and resulted in a Cost of Confusion for which there will never be a satisfactory explanation.

According to the report released by the Texas House of Representatives committee that investigated the tragedy, law enforcement failed utterly in its mission to protect and serve. When the initial reports of the shooting came in, 376 law enforcement officers converged on the school grounds. They represented police and sheriff's departments, the school district, the Texas Rangers, the U.S. Border Patrol, and the Drug Enforcement Agency (DEA).[31]

Meanwhile, inside the school, a small group of first responders gathered in a hall just outside the classroom and debated what to do. The initial moments of uncertainty had a paralyzing effect that compounded the unfolding tragedy. This failure to choose an immediate course of action was cited by the House report as part of "systemic failures and egregiously poor decision-making" by nearly everyone involved. The confusion and repeated delays to act were the results of the decision by the incident commander, school district police chief Pete Arredondo. He chose to treat the scene as a barricaded-person situation rather than as an active-shooter situation. It was a judgment call that further complicated, confused, and delayed the inevitable decision to breach the classroom and take down the shooter.

The agony of parents forced to watch helplessly from across the street is impossible to imagine. They witnessed hundreds of law enforcement officers standing idly by outside the school while waiting for further instructions. Distraught families and the public also dealt with a non-stop flood of inaccurate information that intensified the terror and confusion throughout the town.

The House report cites a laundry list of law enforcement mistakes that expanded far beyond any single commander or agency. The errors were attributed not to a lack of manpower but to an absence of leadership and effective communication. Many of the officers interviewed by the committee admitted they had no idea who was in charge. Several of them described the scene that day as "chaos."

No clear lines of authority, conflicting information, and breakdowns in communication. This is the recurring and tragic theme inherent in a disastrous disaster response. Law enforcement leaders have called for national standards or universal training to prevent a repeat of the deadly confusion at Robb Elementary School.

Fatal Confusion at 30,000 Feet

Two major accidents involving the Boeing 737 MAX aircraft cost the lives of 346 passengers and crew and sparked a long and arduous ordeal for the plane's manufacturer. Confusion lies at the heart of this story as well.

The first tragic accident was the Lion Air Flight 610 crash in Indonesia in October 2018, killing all 189 passengers and crew on board. The investigation into the crash revealed that the cause was a malfunction in the aircraft's flight control system known as MCAS (Maneuvering Characteristics Augmentation System). The system forced the plane's nose to pitch down repeatedly each time the pilot tried to correct it. The crew struggled frantically to understand the problem but ultimately failed to regain control of their aircraft.[32]

The second fatal incident was the crash of Ethiopian Airlines Flight 302 in Ethiopia in March 2019. It resulted in the deaths of all 157 passengers and crew on board. The investigation into this crash revealed that its cause was the same as the previous crash: the MCAS malfunction had caused the plane to pitch down repeatedly despite the crew's efforts.[33]

Root cause analysis focused on erroneous readings from the angle of attack sensors. The sensors indicated the plane was flying not level but nose up. This caused the plane's flight control system to trigger a pitch-down command. The pilot repeatedly pulled the plane up, only to have the autopilot instantly pitch the nose back down.

That fact that two fatal crashes had been caused by flight system data errors pointed the investigations back to potential flaws in design and manufacture. In the process, several other contributing factors came to light.

While I had followed the story, my interest in its potential Cost of Confusion was the result of a conversation with a neighbor who pilots the Boeing 737 MAX for a major American airline. When I mentioned the crashes to him shortly after they happened, he declared, "That would never happen here. Every pilot knows to switch off the AUTOPILOT to deactivate the MCAS."

As I learned later, however, the situation is not as straightforward as that comment suggests. There were two pilot control factors involved. One is recognizing that a malfunctioning MCAS is the likely cause of the plane's sudden, erratic movements. Two is knowing the procedure to disable the MCAS and take over manual control. Neither of these critical factors was universally known or understood among airlines and pilots outside North America and Europe. The reasons stem from decisions Boeing made during the development of the MAX version of the 737 aircraft.[34]

It is standard business practice for aircraft manufacturers to undertake major revamps of current models as a cost-effective alternative to the design of new aircraft. One reason for the strategy is that revamps, unlike new designs, are subject to much less burdensome scrutiny by the Federal Aviation Authority (FAA). Dubbed the 737 MAX, the aircraft had newer, larger engines that were more fuel efficient than previous 737 engines. Associated revisions extended to the design of flight systems, cockpit layouts, pilot controls, and more. Along with changes related to improving performance or reliability, there were others directed at lowering cost. All changes are cycled with the FAA for review and comment.

Included in the MAX changes was the addition of the MCAS maneuvering system. Its purpose was to manage differences in handling introduced by the much larger engines than those on the previous 737 fleet. Designed primarily to address nose-up stalls, the system relied on data input provided by two sensors indicating the angle at which the nose of the plane was pointed up or pointed down.

For manufacturers and the FAA, a key consideration is whether the type and scope of changes will require pilots to take additional training to familiarize themselves with new systems, features, and cockpit controls. Required training takes pilots out of active rotation to spend time in flight simulators at dedicated training facilities. The additional training can add tens of millions of dollars to an airline's cost of acquisition for new planes. This had the potential to cut into Boeing's profit margin on each 737 MAX plane. The potential increased training costs also would complicate the contractual relationships between Boeing and its customers.

It was out of concern over additional training that Boeing employees downplayed the addition of MCAS. The only mention of its function was in a paragraph inserted into the MAX pilot training manual. This would become the driving decision for the cascade of events that led to the deadly crashes.[35]

An undiscovered flaw existed in the design of the MCAS. The input to the system came from two external sensors installed to monitor the position of the plane's nose. What engineers failed to account for was a situation in which one sensor failed or was damaged. Instead of switching to single sensor operation, the system would keep working—but now relying on highly erroneous, conflicting data to control the plane.

In the air, the design flaw had the potential to confuse the MCAS. If it determined there was a risk of a stall, it would activate repeatedly to push down the plane's nose down again and again. This would make it increasingly difficult for pilots to maintain altitude or climb. The system also proved to be confusing to override. Although other crews had successfully managed to do so in similar situations, Lion Air and Ethiopian Airlines flight crews were unable to override the MCAS, resulting in their fatal crashes.

Had more training been required, it is possible that the engineering flaw in the updated flight system might have surfaced and been remedied. Instead, the issue was discovered only after two tragic events. Another factor was the difference in training among pilots flying for major U.S. and European airlines and those flying the airplanes of smaller, less-regulated countries.

In the Indonesian Lion Air crash, the flight crew did not attempt to disable the autopilot. According to the investigation, the crew stayed focused on trying to understand the problem and follow the correct procedures., But they struggled to do so while lacking any awareness of the MCAS system or the brief information provided about it in the aircraft's flight manual.

In the Ethiopian Airlines crash, the flight crew did attempt to disable the autopilot by turning off the electrical trim switches, but they were unable to regain control of the aircraft. According to the investigation, the crew also switched the MCAS system back on. Consequently, it continued to activate, leaving the flight crew unable to counteract its effects.

In this sense, it can be argued that while the design flaw in the MCAS system was a primary cause of the accidents, confusion among the flight crews was a contributing factor that exacerbated the situation and made it impossible for them to regain control of the aircraft. As the emergencies unfolded, both crews likely would have experienced fear and panic that hampered their capacity to think clearly.

In both accidents, the flight crews faced an unexpected and rapidly evolving situation that exceeded their training and experience. These horrific accidents highlight the importance of making flight control changes abundantly clear throughout the industry as well as providing more effective training to ensure safe aviation operations.

Following the multiyear investigation into Boeing's engineering and safety culture, the company completed changes to the 737 MAX flight control system and to the training and information provided to pilots. The Federal Aviation Administration also issued new guidance and requirements for the certification of aircraft and their flight control systems. As of this writing, Boeing continues to negotiate settlements with the surviving families of the crash victims.

Putting Confusion in The Driver's Seat

The National Highway Traffic Safety Administration has determined that 42,915 people died in motor vehicle traffic crashes in 2021. That was a 16-year high and a 10.5% increase from the prior year (NHTSA.gov).[36] Much of the increase is attributed to the widely recognized factors of excessive speed by drivers impaired by alcohol and/or drugs and by drivers distracted by their mobile phones and other onboard electronics. The breakdown of increases by category confirms those factors but also includes some in which confusion may have played a deadly role. These confusion-related causal factors are highlighted by **boldface** type in the list below:

- Fatalities in multi-vehicle crashes up 16%
- **Fatalities on urban roads up 16%**
- **Fatalities among drivers 65 and older up 14%**
- **Pedestrian fatalities up 13%**
- Fatalities in crashes involving at least one large truck up 13%
- **Daytime fatalities up 11%**
- **Motorcyclist fatalities up 9%**
- **Bicyclist fatalities up 5%**
- Fatalities in speeding-related crashes up 5%
- Fatalities in police-reported, alcohol-involvement crashes up 5%

Unfortunately, there is no source of traffic information that identifies fatalities in which confused drivers played a role. However, studies have shown that flawed traffic engineering factors heavily into the root causes of many accidents. The primary culprits are confusing road layouts, unclear lane markings, and poor signage. Here are some details:

- Poor road design—includes roads with confusing or poorly marked lanes, signs that are difficult to understand, or intersections that are complex and difficult to navigate.
  As an example, Portland, Oregon (the author's fair city) has several infamous and dangerous intersections referred to numerically by locals (7Corners, 5Corners, etc.). Periodically, the city holds hearings and proposes redesigns to make these intersections less confusing for drivers and safer for pedestrians. These modifications are perennial works in progress.
- Confusing traffic signals—can leave drivers guessing about what they are supposed to do (merge, yield, wait) or which flow of traffic to follow (straight, must turn, optional turn, etc.)
- Insufficient signage—too few signs to indicate speed limits and poor placement of signs to provide ample time to prepare for exit ramps and highway interchanges
- Complex traffic patterns—increasing use of complex traffic patterns, such as roundabouts or diverging diamond interchanges, that can be difficult for drivers to navigate.
  Another Portland example: the city has completely "redrawn" traffic patterns on hundreds of inner-city streets to carve out dedicated bike lanes. The overlay of lines, arrows, and icons is as confusing to cyclists as it is to motorists. Accidents between bikes and cars has increased in some of these re-jiggered intersections. The city has failed to communicate clearly to either group about how to safely navigate this new network.

The risk of accidents due to these factors is especially acute for older drivers and those who are new to an area. The same is true for drivers who are already distracted or impaired. This is the deadly confusion that results in cars careening across three lanes for a last-minute exit or slowing down to decipher a complex highway interchange. At the extreme are those motorists who blindly enter exit ramps and cluelessly drive into head-on traffic.

In fairness to traffic engineers, many of the problems are legacy issues related to the age of roads and highways that were designed and built before "safety by design" thinking evolved to the point it is today. Currently, the federal government is taking major steps to update the country's neglected infrastructure and improve public safety.

In May 2022, U.S. Transportation Secretary Pete Buttigieg took aim at the increased number of traffic fatalities in the prior year. "With our National Roadway Safety Strategy and the President's Bipartisan Infrastructure Law, we are taking critical steps to help reverse this devastating trend and save lives on our roadways."[36]

The Bipartisan Infrastructure Law now being implemented puts new emphasis on policies and standards for traffic engineering intended to reduce confusion for drivers. Also included are updates to the Manual on Uniform Traffic Control Devices, which defines speeds, standardizes lane markings, traffic lights, and more on most roads in the country. Furthermore, it significantly increases funding for the Highway Safety Improvement Program, which helps states adopt data-driven approaches to making roads safer—and less confusing.

Operator Error

Despite a highly layered network of agencies and organizations devoted to consumer product safety, the risks posed by confusion remain. There are several classes of consumer products that are susceptible to these risks, leading to high rates of accidents, injuries, and sometimes fatalities.

- Baby products—products such as cribs, play yards, strollers, and car seats can pose a risk of suffocation, entrapment, or injury if they have been assembled incorrectly or used/installed improperly
- Children's toys and products—parents and caregivers can fail to understand the risk of choking, suffocation, or injury if children are not supervised while playing with these products
- Home appliances and furniture—products such as space heaters, stoves, ovens, and furniture can pose a risk of fire, electrocution, or injury if owners ignore or misunderstand important safety instructions
- Sports .and recreation equipment—products such as bicycles, skateboards, and sporting equipment can pose a risk of injury if assembled incorrectly, used without protective gear, or under unsafe conditions
- Power tools and machinery—perhaps the most dangerous category of consumer products; misuse of power tools, lawnmowers, and chainsaws puts users at risk of traumatic injuries that can include loss of fingers, toes, hands, or worse

These are just a few examples of the types of products for which the Cost of Confusion can be measured by the rates of accidents, injuries, and fatalities.

Sometimes, the first indication arrives too late. Too frequently, it is only through a safety recall that the role of confusion in product-related fatalities comes to light. Some of the most high-profile cases have involved products intended for infants and young children. Sometimes, these recalls reveal the fatal consequences that can result when parents and caregivers have been confused about the intended use of a product and its possible hazards. [sometimes they are just plain bad products]

In 2019, the Consumer Products Safety Commission (CPSC) issued a recall of a popular infant swing associated with more than 100 reports of suffocation.[37] The design used non-breathable fabric for the seat pocket, that posed a risk that was not widely understood. For the swing to be used safely, it was essential that babies remained on their backs while on the swings. Many parents and caregivers were unaware of this risk that required them to constantly monitor their baby's position. Tragically, some unattended infants managed to roll over and were trapped face down. Unable to breathe because of the fabric, these babies suffocated.

Beyond recalls, there have been many cases of accidental poisoning attributed to toxic dishwasher tablets that look like candy. Other incidents involved confusion over product packaging, resulting in young children eating teething gels and creams meant for topical use.

To help prevent these and other avoidable incidents, consumers and manufacturers must share the responsibility for safety.

- Manufacturers must design safety into these products, keep defective products from reaching the marketplace, and clearly communicate all relevant safety information and instructions for using their products.
- Consumers who purchase these products owe it to themselves and their families to take safe usage seriously. This means reading instructions first and heeding the warnings provided by the manufacturer.

The is also a role for consumer protection agencies. Their attempts to impose safety on manufacturers is a major reason so many people do not read the directions and safety warnings.

When buyers open the printed instructions and see the first three pages devoted to legalese, disclaimers, and warnings that insult the person of average intelligence, the instructions get tossed back in the box. To counter this risky behavior, protection agencies and industries should look to information designers. There is a need and an opportunity to rethink the content and design of instructions and safety information. Adding three more warning labels to the AC cord is not a solution.

The instances where Confusion has led to fatal consequences far exceed the examples explored in this chapter. For example, America's and the world's industrial workforces face hazardous conditions every day. According to the U.S. Bureau of Labor statistics, workers in the U.S. experienced 5,190 fatal work injuries in 2021. From chemical plants, refineries, and steel mills to manufacturing plants, commercial construction, and more, there are no guarantees of safety—but eliminating confusion goes a long way in keeping every workplace as safe as it can be.

Chapter 7

Eliminating Confusion: A Methodology

As the prior chapters have demonstrated, confusion is ubiquitous. It is, however, not obvious because it exists only in the minds of employees, voters, customers, and patients. The closest it comes to being observable is by way of puzzled expressions and collective head-scratching.

The good news is that the presence of confusion can be established if we know where to look. A wide range of behaviors and characteristics provide a pretty good indication of underlying failures to communicate. Consider these examples.

- **Recurring questions.** Are the same questions being asked over and over in orientation, training, or sales presentations? How about questions asked at customer service desks or coming into inbound call centers? Frequently Asked Questions (FAQs) indicate that important pieces of information may be missing or that current explanations are ineffective.
- **Disappointing Metrics.** Sales volumes that lag forecasts, productivity that falls short of industry benchmarks, abandoned online shopping carts, high rates of customer returns of products in perfect condition—these are metrics that can indicate people are not "getting it." There is some aspect of the value proposition, work process, or technology that people do not grasp.
- **Unhappy Campers.** Negative attitudes and behaviors among groups experiencing organizational change indicate that not everyone is on board with new ways of working. Increased conflict, lackadaisical performance, doing things the "old way," and other passive-aggressive behaviors can mask a lack of understanding around the business case for change.

There are no special skills involved. It just requires paying closer attention and using a slightly different lens through which to view the everyday

DOI: 10.4324/9781003301080-7

world. Be forewarned, however, that you will never see the world the same way again!

How to Cut The Cost of Confusion

I began my checkered career in the field of marketing communications (marcom). This is a corporate function that does not include a "seat at the table" with executive leadership. Typically, the role is that of a glorified order taker. It puts you at the mercy of people who know nothing about your professional discipline but nevertheless feel entitled to tell you how to do your job—and then blame you when the results the results they want are not forthcoming!

Suffice to say, it was a soul-sucking day job. Fortunately, self-preservation sent me out the door on a path to gain more control and deliver greater value. After setting up shop as Transform Communications, I began a series of consulting engagements that enabled me to develop a practical methodology inspired by Transform's tagline, *Cutting the Cost of Confusion.*

This disciplined, strategic methodology brings confusion out into the open, helps quantify its risks, and provides a blueprint to mitigate confusion's impact. The methodology integrates four functions into a unique form of Risk Management. It is best suited for use by professionals in marketing communications, advertising, graphic design, training, and organizational development. The most effective application harnesses their multi-discipline expertise in a designated team. Team members work collaboratively to implement the methodology and produce the wide range of content and tools that will be needed. Following a brief overview of the component parts and activities, I will walk through an in-depth application example.

| Stakeholder Risk Management | Engagement Strategy | Information Architecture | Knowledge Management |

Figure 7.1

Stakeholder   Engagement   Information   Knowledge
Risk Management   Strategy   Architecture   Management

Figure 7.2

STAKEHOLDER RISK MANAGEMENT

The success of every organization is dependent upon *stakeholders*. These are the various parties that have an interest based on their ability to affect the organization (e.g., workers, members, etc.) or to be affected by it (customers, shareholders, etc.). Within each group of stakeholders are people who can make or break success according to the roles they have, the decisions they make, and the behaviors they display. Stakeholders present risks to success.

The first step in the methodology is to assess the organization's vulnerability to confusion across the stakeholder audience within the context of a desired outcome. For example, if the goal is launching a new business software product, key internal stakeholder groups are the product development team and the marketing sales department. Key external stakeholder groups are IT managers in the target market and business technology media outlets.

> ### Analyze Stakeholder Groups
>
> - Identify groups with a "make-or-break" impact
> - Consider obstacles/threats each group presents
> - Assess each group's "need-to-know" and the consistent behaviors needed to ensure the desired business outcome

A powerful visual exercise for this step is **stakeholder mapping**. This is a technique used to brainstorm potential stakeholders, categorize them, and identify linkages and relationships. Categories to consider include:

- **Customers/User Groups**: the intended users of products and services (can be internal or external); they may be the purchasers as well
- **Economic buyers**: generally, this is the customer but also can be a higher-level authority who approves a purchase decision

- **Recommenders:** people sufficiently knowledgeable to evaluate a product, service, policy, or political candidate and provide input to decision-makers
- **Influencers:** groups whose opinions, behaviors, and networks
- **Partners:** groups with a mutual interest in the organization's success; can include resellers, dealers, service companies, etc.
- **Regulators:** groups that have government or licensing authority over an organization and how it operates

STAKEHOLDER DYNAMICS

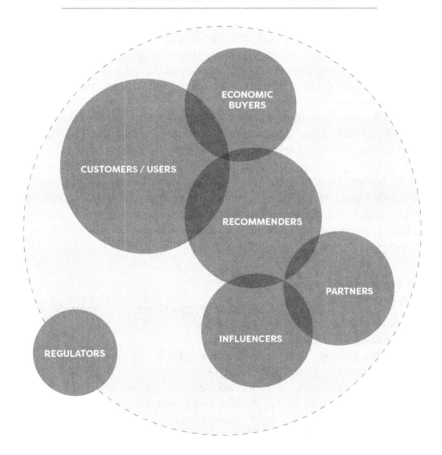

Figure 7.3

Stakeholder **Engagement** Information Knowledge
Risk Management **Strategy** Architecture Management

Figure 7.4

Once the stakeholder universe has been identified, the next step is assessing the risk that each group presents if it does not "get with the program." Each group has its own set of perceptions, opinions, biases, and other factors influencing them. Some groups will present obstacles, while others have the power to be show-stoppers. The latter include customers and economic buyers as well as regulators. Recommenders, influencers, and others have the power to inhibit results but are not so critical to success. Within an organization, identify the specific "gatekeepers" who have the potential to impact success.

Typically, the compelling reasons for buying or buying into the organization's agenda differ across the stakeholder audience. This means analyzing each group in terms of familiarity, knowledge, opinions, prejudices, prior experience, and more to determine what individuals within that group will need to understand. This analysis is a means of fostering desired decisions and behaviors. The goal of this analysis is to identify the key pieces of information that will need to be strategically clarified, packaged and communicated to the various stakeholder individuals and groups.

ENGAGEMENT STRATEGY

Information can foster understanding among stakeholder groups, but it cannot provide motivation and inspiration. The ability to articulate "What's in it for me?" to the members of

Foster Inspiration and Provide Incentive

- Engage people in the vision for success
- Focus on "what's in it for me?"
- Clarify the stakes & opportunities
- Manage expectations

each group is key to aligning stakeholders with the organization's goals. Whether it's about buying, buying in, or buying time, engagement is the way organizations connect with people and build relationships over time. The engagement strategy is the foundation.

Engaging internal audiences (e.g., employees) begins by crafting a shared vision for success, one that conveys not only the upside of opportunities, but alsoconveys the risks of failure. Making a clear case for why something is important not only to the upper ranks of the organization, but also to the entire workforce is something very rarely done well, if at all. This step leads to a strategy for reaching all stakeholders.

For external stakeholder groups (e.g., customers), this exercise is less clear cut. Generally, conveying the benefits is what engages potential buyers. They don't risk failure, but they do have pain points to address. This is where compelling value propositions come in. Look for more on this in the sidebar and in the case study later in the chapter.

The information gleaned from the previous step is used to develop a set of key messages tailored to resonate uniquely with their respective stakeholder groups. The point of messaging is to have a consistent set of answers to the classic questions—"Who?" "What?" Why?

Key messages are the core of communications, marketing, advertising, and change efforts. Management and other professional disciplines rely on succinct, repeatable messages to educate, inform, address objections, and foster desired behaviors. Sustainable organizations never stop engaging stakeholders and proactively managing relationships with and among them.

A master stakeholder messaging document typically includes four types of information:

1. Key messages: a list of the most important points each audience needs to hear/understand
2. Objections: the challenging questions most often asked by each audience
3. Responses: a matched set of well-reasoned, persuasive responses to each objection
4. Proof points: easily grasped evidence that can be used to further neutralize challenges

Details on putting together a stakeholder messaging document are covered in Chapter 8, Application and Case Studies.

Snapshot: Rethinking the True Buyer

The chainsaw is the most dangerous powered hand tool in the world. In the U.S. alone, it is responsible for an average of 36,000 emergency room visits each year. Many of the injuries are life-altering, especially those caused by a phenomenon known as "kickback." Without warning, the moving blade jumps out of the cut and swings in a split-second back toward the operator. Serious wounds to the head and torso can result.

A small company set out to eliminate kickback injuries by bringing an ingenious chainsaw safety device to the consumer market. The Centurion™ was a bolt-on steel bar that put a mechanical barrier between the cutting teeth of the saw and the user. When a kickback occurred, the steel guard prevented injuries to the operator. Explaining how the guard worked was an essential part of the rollout, but stakeholder assessment revealed some surprising opportunities for the marketing strategy.

The end user group was primarily male and was categorized as the *economic buyer* as well, but there was a prevailing attitude that "real men don't use chainsaw guards." Consequently, advertising directly to this group had minimal impact on initial sales. Surprisingly, the stakeholders with whom chainsaw safety resonated the most turned out to be *influencers:* wives, daughters, and granddaughters. Shifting the marketing campaign to focus on this group had a significant impact on sales of not only the chainsaw guard but also of other safety-related accessories displayed alongside it in stores.

Stakeholder analysis also revealed a group that could be leveraged in the marketing campaign as *recommenders:* professional loggers. Although they did not consider the product for themselves, they recognized the benefits for non-professional users and were willing to endorse The Centurion as a must-have safety device for weekend chainsaw warriors.

Following the early launch of the product, a follow-up stakeholder exercise revealed a *regulatory agency* with the potential to be a game-changer for The Centurion. The Consumer Products Safety Commission (CPSC) has a long history of landmark decrees that have forced product manufacturers to improve the safety of their products. With a one final "sale" to the CPSC, The Centurion essentially could become the seat belt of the chainsaw industry!

Unfortunately, the fledgling effort to engage the CPSC brought out the industry's lawyers and lobbyists in droves. Their argument was that incorporating a chainsaw guard into their products would be a de facto admission that all prior chainsaws sold had a dangerous safety flaw. The resulting class action product liability lawsuits would be devastating to chainsaw manufacturers and their dealer networks. Sadly, the resistance from this deep-pocketed group of stakeholders that we had overlooked was too powerful to overcome. The pressure from manufacturers began to close off sales outlets and, eventually, put the makers of The Centurion out of business.

Stakeholder   Engagement   **Information**   Knowledge
Risk Management   Strategy   **Architecture**   Management

Figure 7.5

INFORMATION ARCHITECTURE

The journey from confusion to understanding is, essentially, a learning process. The mind makes its way (or is led) through a body of information, taking in concepts, ideas, and definitions until they add up to a firm and accurate grasp of the subject. There are no limitations on where that journey takes place or how much time it will require to complete. It can happen in minutes in a store aisle, in hours at a computer, in days during training classes, or in months in a workplace.

Making that journey as easy and intuitive as possible for people depends on how the required body of information is structured, i.e., its **information architecture**.

It's no coincidence that a variety of architectural metaphors are applied to learning, as all learning takes place by building upon previously acquired knowledge. There are cornerstones and foundations, building blocks, supporting pillars, doorways, pathways, bridges, handles, stairways, and levels. As part of the methodology for cutting the cost of confusion, information architecture is the practice of structuring information so that it is accessible and organized in meaningful categories and a logical hierarchy of detail. It centers on making the complex clear and useful.

Developing the architecture begins with an information audit to determine what is required to communicate with and engage each stakeholder group. What does each need to see, hear, and understand, and what is the step-by-step blueprint to accomplish that?

In some ways, it is like developing a college curriculum, considering how to carve up a body of knowledge into course levels 101, 201, and 301. Each is a prerequisite for the next.

> **Make the complex clear and useful**
>
> - Determine the prerequisite foundation for learning
> - Develop conceptual structure for content
> - Visualize workflows/organizational links
> - Communicate the Big Picture and multiple levels of detail

- 101—content typically included in introduction/overview, e.g., core principles, key concepts, definitions, and other foundational content to help others recognize why they should buy or buy in
- 201—the basics of form, function, features, benefits, roles, and responsibilities; this level fosters engagement and helps to sustain business initiatives
- 301—the detailed "user's manual"—content for practitioners, operators, technical contributors—all of those who will have hands-on, everyday interaction with complex products, technologies, processes, and business models.

The information architecture results in a logical taxonomy (aka structured body of knowledge) that enables people to approach it initially from a bird's-eye view and then "drill down" to the appropriate levels of detail needed to fulfill their individual roles and responsibilities.

The following example illustrates a taxonomy used to develop SharePoint web portal.

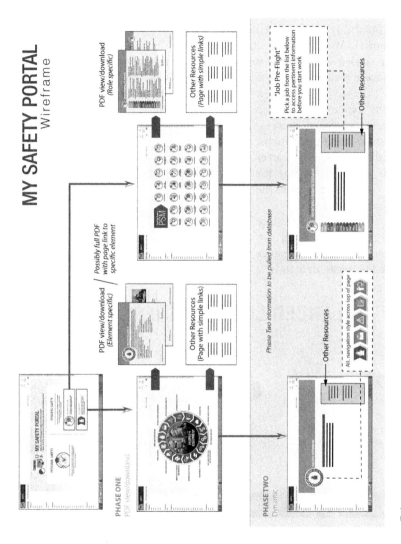

Figure 7.6

Beyond Words

Rationally organizing a body of complex information adds tremendous value in terms of its capacity to be accessed, understood, and applied toward a desired end. Not everyone learns by reading or listening, so relying on words alone is only part of developing an effective information architecture. The ability to visualize key concepts, processes, and workflows adds exponential value. Not only does this address the needs of those with visual learning styles, but also creates powerful tools that increase the speed of information transfer across the workforce. "A picture is worth a thousand words," the saying goes. A well-designed information graphic can replace a lengthy explanation, saving time in a world of increasingly short attention spans. The addition of a short, clever caption such as this one for Figure 7.7 can enhance the communication impact.

This is not a call for more PowerPoint slides and clip art, however. A high-performance knowledge base demands a

Caption:

WHEN IT COMES TO PROJECTS, WE CAN HAVE *ANYTHING* – BUT WE CAN'T HAVE *EVERYTHING!*

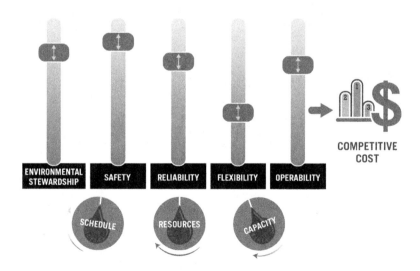

BALANCED COST BUSINESS CASE

Figure 7.7

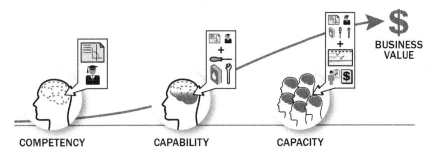

COMPETENCY   CAPABILITY   CAPACITY

Figure 7.8

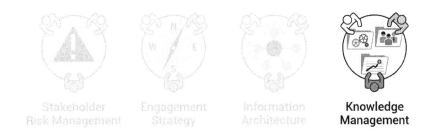

Stakeholder   Engagement   Information   **Knowledge**
Risk Management   Strategy   Architecture   **Management**

Figure 7.9

high impact, professionally designed visual interface. The design style, color palette, font choices, photo composition and other visual elements should align closely with corporate brand guides while conveying a sense of identity within the organization.

Consider these examples of information graphics and icons. Note that not all are self-explanatory due to the complexity of the concepts they represent. Rather, they are used to support explanations and enhance "speed-to-know."

KNOWLEDGE MANAGEMENT

By itself, an information taxonomy/body of knowledge has no practical value to an organization. It takes people to access and apply or act upon that information to unlock its value. This

Deliver the Right Information at the Right Level to the Right People at the Right Time

- Design stakeholder-matched content
- Deliver information when and where it is needed
- Incorporate a variety of channels and media

is the final stage in the Cutting the Cost of Confusion Methodology—creating and deploying content at the optimum level using the appropriate media mix for each stakeholder group. The media mix draws from traditional print, online, video, in-person, and interactive platforms and now extends to social media, virtual environments, and beyond.

The touchpoints and environments are also considered when designing and packaging content. Sales and marketing materials are deployed via direct mail, point-of-purchase displays, billboards, email, and online advertising. Corporate initiatives have a different mix—break rooms and coffee stations, dedicated intranets, stand-up meetings and training, video messages from the CEO, etc. Being strategic about the how, where, when, what, and to whom, is the essence of effective knowledge management.

The primary mistake, most organizations make is Information Overload. The software sales team presents all 25 features to every potential customer, no matter how many in the audience are yawning and checking their watches. Reality is that customers base their buying decisions on subsets of features, and those subsets will differ. IT Managers only care about features 3, 7 and 10. Programmers are most intrigued by features 2, 5, and 19. The purchasing manager may not care at all. The ability to tailor each interaction to the three or four features that each stakeholder group truly values is vital to closing the sale.

Similarly, all employees do not need to read and understand the user manual of the new technology platform the company has just rolled out. Executives need only a high-level understanding of how the company will benefit to play their part—expressing an all-important show of support. Managers and supervisors need a functional understanding to support their teams. It is only hands-on users who need to be educated and trained to become highly proficient operators/technicians.

The goal of this methodology is to give each key audience a reason to care about, engage with and commit to mindful application of business processes, information resources, and tools. Or, in the case of customers, giving each a reason to buy your products and engage with your company.

Following are example graphics that highlight the scope of typical knowledge bases and indicate how their components function within their overall taxonomies.

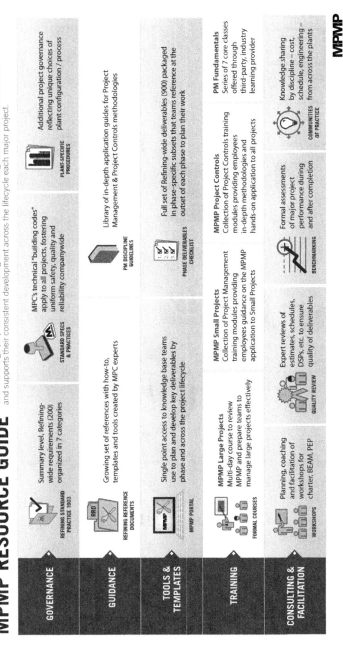

Figure 7.10

Description: *A visual designed for employees to see at-a-glance the complete inventory of available guidelines and tools they will use to apply a global management process.*

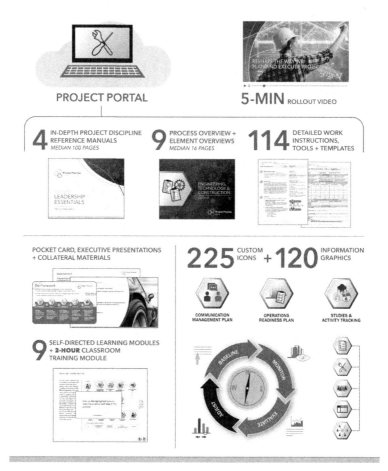

Figure 7.11

Description: *The scope of a typically integrated knowledge base for global enterprise organizations*

Wash, Rinse, Repeat

Following the initial application, this methodology should become an ongoing internal capability that is integrated into strategic decision-making, large-scale technology rollouts, product development, and any other critical business initiatives. Organizations that give savvy communicators a seat the table early on get a powerful new lens through which to assess and manage risk, better engage people, and deliver desired results.

QUICK START GUIDE: *Cost of Confusion Methodology*

Follow this disciplined, strategic framework for identifying / quantifying risks and preventing failures to communicate.

**Stakeholder
Risk Management**

Figure 7.12

Analyze Stakeholder Groups
- Identify groups with "make-or-break" impact
- Consider obstacles/threats each group presents
- Assess each group's "need-to-know" and the consistent behaviors needed to ensure desired business outcome

**Engagement
Strategy**

Figure 7.13

Foster Inspiration and Provide Incentive
- Engage people in the vision for success
- Focus on "what's in it for me?"
- Clarify the stakes & opportunities
- Manage expectations

**Information
Architecture**

Figure 7.14

Make the complex clear and useful
- Determine prerequisite foundation for learning
- Develop conceptual structure for content
- Visualize workflows/organizational links
- Communicate both Big Picture and multiple levels of detail

**Knowledge
Management**

Figure 7.15

Deliver the Right Information to the Right People at the Right Time
- Design stakeholder-matched content
- Deliver information when it is needed
- Incorporate a variety of channels and media

Chapter 8

Applying the Methodology

Here's a chance to roll up your sleeves and head deep into a practical application of the methodology. It's my hope that following the detailed thought process will demystify this work and inspire readers to give it try. It's simply an exercise in diligent thinking.

THE SITUATION
Vats of Bubbling Hot Tar
An Industry Stuck in Time
Tar, asphalt, and bitumen have been the staples of waterproofing and roofing for thousands of years. These thick, highly viscous hydrocarbons occur naturally in oil and gas formations and are now derived from commercial oil refining. Historically, the primary method for applying these materials in commercial flat-roofed buildings consisted of alternating layers of fabric and tar topped by gravel. Application involved lifting buckets by rope and then manually mopping their contents uniformly across each layer of fabric. To finish the job, roofers sprinkled gravel across the sticky surface. This helped reflect heat and protect the underlying material from degrading due to ultraviolet radiation. Known as "Built-up Roofing" (BUR), this product dominated commercial construction well into the 20th Century.

Materials research in Italy led to the development of a lighter, easier-to-apply product known as Modified Bitumen Roofing (MB). It is produced by saturating a super tensile fabric sheet with a bitumen solution to which plastics and rubber have been added. Colored mineral granules are applied prior to curing and packaging the sheets into rolls for shipping. Application requires the use of a propane torch to heat up the underside of the material as it is rolled out. This effectively bonds the material to the roof deck. Rolls are overlapped and bonded as well, creating a one-piece waterproofing "membrane" on the roof.

Modified bitumen was a game-changer for the commercial roofing industry in Europe, but the weight of the product made shipping to North America prohibitively expensive. A small manufacturer of sheet metal supplies in

DOI: 10.4324/9781003301080-8

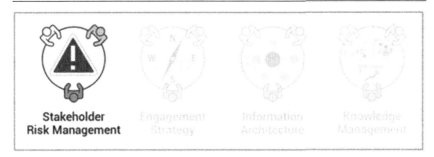

Stakeholder
Risk Management

Figure 8.1

Texas licensed the technology and set out to introduce modified bitumen roofing to the massive US market. I was privileged to assist in that endeavor.

It was obvious there would be a steep learning curve involved, as there had never been a reason to differentiate between generic building materials that are black, sticky, heavy, and applied using heat. The products all looked alike and were applied in the same way; that meant education would be the core of the marketing strategy, with every element geared toward *cutting the cost of confusion*.

Stakeholder Assessment

This first step involved identifying anyone and everyone who has the power to impede widespread product acceptance, create friction in distribution channels and limit sales. The order in which the stakeholders are listed is not a reflection of importance, as there are many facets to product launch and sales—and any stakeholder can be a point of entry to the overall sales cycle. This exercise also contributes to determining the scope of the marketing system. There should be "something for everyone"—one or more pieces of promotional material, dedicated website pages, ad campaigns, and more to present targeted messages to each stakeholder group.

Stakeholder	*Nature of Involvement*	*Role(s)*
Regulatory Agencies (OSHA, ASTD, etc.)	Gatekeepers and potential showstoppers whose approval is needed to enable building products to be marketed and sold in the first place; approval also impacts insurability of contractors and projects	Approvers (no sale without them!)

Stakeholder	Nature of Involvement	Role(s)
Local Permitting Authorities and Fire Depts.	Second tier of gatekeepers, they determine whether roofing products and systems meet applicable local / county building codes; generally, the most stringent codes (e.g., Florida) are applied to manufacturing	Approvers (no sale without them!)
Building Owners & Commercial Developers	Ultimate "buyers" of the roofing system, though rarely the party making the purchasing decision; can direct others (architects, contractors) as to the type of roofing products / manufacturers to be used	Requestors Specifiers Purchasers
Roofing Contractors	Primary purchasers of roofing materials for the projects they bid on; concerns are quality and reliability, but margin is also important	Purchasers Recommenders
Roofers / Installers	Product / roof performance ultimately depends on how well these workers are trained and motivated to install the product correctly and safely on every roof they tackle	Direct Users Quality Assurance
Distributors & Dealers	Control market access through decisions to stock products and promote them to customers; affected by product quality, margin/perks	Resellers Recommenders
Architects	Building designers who, historically, had been constrained by flat roofing systems; modified products open up new creative possibilities for dramatic roof designs	Specifiers Recommenders Influencers

Stakeholder	Nature of Involvement	Role(s)
Engineers	Licensed professionals who turn designs into executable drawings that ensure structural integrity, safety and conformance to code	Specifiers Recommenders
Specifiers	Contractor role that develops lists of approved suppliers and building materials to be used in construction projects	Specifiers
Procurement Professionals	Guided by approved supplier lists and specifications, this group manages bulk purchases of building materials	Approvers Purchasers
Commercial Insurers	Issue policies providing coverage against catastrophic loss, construction liability and structural damage; rates and claims can be affected by choice of roofing systems and installation	Underwriters Recommenders Influencers
Industry Associations	Organizations that foster knowledge sharing within the roofing and building materials industries offer forums in which to promote technology advances and establish credibility	Influencers
Industry Press	Media companies and publishers that serve all sectors of commercial development and manufacturing; also roofing specific press outlets will be leveraged for company and product PR and advertising	Influencers

Notes on this exercise.

It helps to convene a wide range of participants when kicking off stake-holder analysis. Focus on the diversity of their experience and knowledge about how markets operate and how regulations, relationships, and other factors may impact the organization's desired business goals.

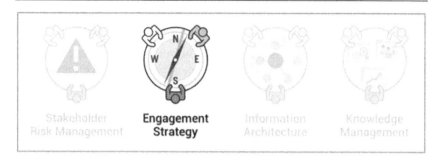

Stakeholder
Risk Management

**Engagement
Strategy**

Information
Architecture

Knowledge
Management

Figure 8.2

Personal Engagement

Each stakeholder identified in step one represents both an opportunity and a degree of risk. If each group and all its members think that modified bitumen roofing is the greatest thing since sliced bread, then we're done! Nothing left to do but make sales. That, of course, was not the case, and never is.

Preparation for this next step involves focusing on the UVP (Unique Value Proposition). This is a succinct summary of what makes a product or service valuable to its intended users and how that value is "unique" compared to competing offerings in the market. The differentiated value proposition developed for modified bitumen roofing centered on three key benefits:

1. MB formulation outperforms conventional BUR: polyester fabric core and elastic polymers provide greater flexibility, tensile strength, and temperature resistance that equate to longer service life.
2. MB Installation with its single-layer roll on/torch-down application method is faster, easier, and less labor intensive than the conventional hot mop method for BUR.
3. MB means more freedom for architects because, unlike BUR, the membrane can be applied to sloped roofs, is lighter weight and comes in a greater range of colors.

These benefits formed the basis of the core messaging. Each message is then tailored for greater impact with the various stakeholder audiences and to drive personal engagement with individual stakeholders.

The universal tool used for this exercise is a messaging matrix. It aligns stakeholders, concerns, and tailored messages in a single reference document. This ensures everyone is "on the same page" while developing marketing, PR, advertising, and other communications over time.

Stakeholder	Concerns	Key Message
Regulatory Agencies (OSHA, ASTD, etc.) Local Permitting Authorities and Fire Depts.	Meets standards for safety, weather / wind resistance, flame resistance, strength, reliability	Modified bitumen roofing membrane is a proven roofing product that has been used widely throughout Europe. The products we manufacture meet and/or exceed the most stringent requirements across the US Hazards associated with torch application (open flame) are minimized through use of rigorous procedures for installation safety and quality assurance
Building Owners & Commercial Developers	Upfront cost, property value, service life, maintenance, warranty	Exceptional price/value. Our products have a higher upfront cost than traditional BUR, but they outperform those roofing systems to provide lower cost of ownership. In addition, they enable upscale design features and are covered by an iron-clad warranty
Roofing Contractors	Project margins, product liability, no call-backs to fix problems	Our MB roofing systems give contractors a competitive edge thanks to faster installation and bigger job margins; Contractors can offer their customers innovative roofing options and greater piece of mind.
Roofers / Installers	Products that are simple/easy to work with	Roofing systems are only as good as the people installing them. We depend on the skilled expertise of our roofing partners to deliver the most important part of every roof: Confidence!
Distributors & Dealers	Margins, trusted manufacturer, exclusivity	We value strong relationships with distributors and dealers, offering them exclusive access to superior roofing products and the higher margins they command.

Stakeholder	Concerns	Key Message
Architects	Greater design freedom, roof integrity	MB roofing is the product architects have been waiting for to let their imaginations—and their rooflines—soar! Dramatic visual appeal coupled with superior waterproofing and wind resistance.
Engineers	Structural integrity, conformance to code, safety	MB roofing systems are certified by ASTM (American Society for Testing and Materials) and meet the standards of the most stringent municipal construction codes (e.g., Dade County, FL)
Specifiers	Guaranteed performance	MB roofing systems meet / exceed all applicable construction and permitting requirements for commercial projects
Procurement Professionals	Price/value, availability, warranty	Our MB roofing systems are performance, widely available through a robust network of distributors and dealers and backed by the strongest warranty in the industry
Commercial Insurers	systems and installation	High performance MB roofing systems stand up to wind and weather extremes to offer superior protection against damage
Industry Associations	Advances in roofing and building materials, conference sales	MB roofing systems are expanding the possibilities and the opportunities within the industry by introducing new technologies and competitive advantages.
Industry Press	Sales of advertising, newsworthy innovation	MB roofing systems are shaking up the traditional roofing industry and creating new opportunities for contractors, architects and dealers

Notes on this exercise.
Congratulations! If you have taken a deep dive into the messaging matrix, you are on your way to mastering the art of tailoring value propositions to match a broad range of "hot button" concerns. For extra credit, the matrix can be expanded to include primary objections and responses.

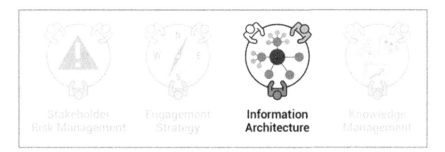

Stakeholder
Risk Management

Engagement
Strategy

**Information
Architecture**

Knowledge
Management

Figure 8.3

Information Architecture

This step involves setting up the intellectual framework/knowledge base from which all stakeholder communications are developed. Given that education would be central to the successful launch of modified bitumen roofing in the U.S. market, the task was to outline the information progression needed to drive understanding.

Foundation Concepts are those that everyone must grasp first – before they can move on to deeper learning. This is the 101 course of MB roofing technology focusing on *formulation* and *application*—the two primary differentiators from conventional roofing.

The essence of *formulation* is the addition of engineered polymers to the tar/bitumen raw material. Blending in selected long-chain plastic molecules imparts elasticity, flexibility, and the wide temperature tolerance that define MB performance characteristics. The polyester fabric sheet at the core serves as the base layer for the mixture and provides the extreme tensile strength. Along with concise verbal descriptions, a set of key illustrations provided visual support, depicting the molecules, center sheet, and colored granules. A two-dimensional (2D) cutaway illustration conveyed the contrast between MB and Built-Up Roofing systems. The foundation set of branded graphics was leveraged across all media, including print, web, video animation, and trade show display.

The essence of *application* was a little easier to explain and demonstrate. The material is heat bonded to the roof surface through the use of a high temperature propane torch head. The configuration of the head concentrates the flame on the underside of the roll while the roofer works to distribute heat evenly across the face of the material as it drops onto the roof deck. At the same time, the heated edge bonds to the top edge of the adjacent roll so that the finished job results in a leak-free roof membrane on top of the structure. Supporting visuals include action photos and a video of installation. Detailed graphics illustrated how the rolls are overlapped, and edges are finished to complete the roof. The visual assets would be leveraged not only in marketing and advertising, but also for training.

With the basics outlined, the next components in the architecture focused on articulating and compiling information according to business objectives.

- For regulators and technical audiences: product specifications and performance data
- For marketing and sales: a repository of information to drive selling conversations in terms of features/advantages/benefits
- For installation: definitive "how to" instructions to cover every aspect of safety, quality, and long-term roof integrity

Notes on this exercise.
The completed information architecture should contain the knowledge to answer every possible question a stakeholder could ask, from the highest to the lowest level of detail. It serves as the set of construction blueprints for the buildout of marketing communications material and provides an immediate resource for development of Frequently Asked Questions to add to a website or other media. Expect the knowledge base to evolve as new FAQs emerge and stakeholders' concerns shift.

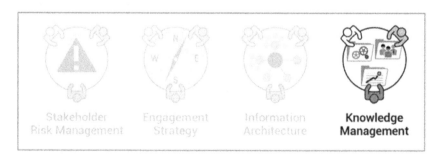

Stakeholder Risk Management   Engagement Strategy   Information Architecture   **Knowledge Management**

Figure 8.4

Knowledge Management

Typically, organizations fall into one of two faulty communication modes: providing people with too little relevant information or too much irrelevant information. The typical broadcast approach distributes the same information to everyone and garners minimal engagement as a result. Nothing loses an audience faster than information its members don't need or can't act upon. Without relevance, information is just more noise to tune out.

This step of the methodology leverages the knowledge base to maximize the value of the information it contains. The approach is simple: deliver the right information at the right level in the right format to the right person at the right time.

A feature of this industry—commodity construction materials—is that a potential sale can be initiated at a variety of points within the market ecosystem. This called for a very purpose-driven approach to planning, design, and production of the integrated marketing communications system. Here are examples of items in the inventory of collateral.

- For specifiers and engineers: technical packets containing detailed testing data, typical application drawings, MSDS (Material Safety Data Sheets), and more
- For owners and architects: color brochures and slide decks featuring "beauty shots" of premium high-rise offices, luxury hotels, and other commercial developments featuring dramatic architectural roof designs
- For distributors: point-of-purchase displays and counter cards to create product awareness
- For contractors and installers: step-by-step procedure manuals and video training modules

Another mechanism for matching information to the stakeholder group was development of role-based navigation on the company's website. This enabled site visitors to self-identify their roles (e.g., contractor, specifier, architect, etc.) and follow a clickstream through tailored messages and relevant technical information.

Ultimately, the marcom system was fully assembled with all components aligned to the sales cycle. Regardless of where a selling conversation might start—at conferences, trade shows, board rooms, job sites, architects' offices, distributor warehouses, or somewhere else, the system had specific components to move prospects step by step and close the sale.

Sales Toolbox

Majestic Sampleboards

Description: 24" Sampleboards for Legend, Sundance and Royalwood shingles—includes color samples, one full-width shingle and a customer benefits overview.

Literature Reorder:
Royalwood   MS-101.1
Sundance   MS-101.2
Legend   MS-101.3

MAJESTIC

PREMIUM
RESIDENTIAL
ROOFING

Majestic Yard Signs

Description: 18" x 24" vinyl yard sign for placement in customer's yard prior to and during roofing job. Allows contractor to canvas neighborhood, knock on doors and leave door hangers calling attention to the roofing job in their neighborhood.

Literature Reorder: MS-103
Custom-print your Firm's name;
$3 per sign, minimum order: 12.

Majestic Presentation Folder

Description: 9" x 12" 2-pocket folder with business card slot. Holds complete proposal with sales literature.

Literature Reorder: MS-104
May be custom-printed with your Firm's
name on front cover; 75¢ per folder,
minimum order: 200.

Example | **County Roofing Co**
Text | **Serving the East Slope Since 1900**

Majestic Door Hanger

Description: 4 ¼" x 11" door hanger with 1 ¼ hole for door knob. Blanket neighborhoods in conjunction with local advertising, while doing a job nearby or following a weatherstorm.

Literature Reorder: MS-105

Figure 8.5

The Outcome

The company's founder, a self-described "good old boy," insisted that the logo design include an icon of a Texas jackrabbit to characterize how fast the company took off. A steady run of double-digit sales growth attracted a lot of industry attention to this small manufacturer. The company enjoyed a few years as a sales leader thanks to its first-mover advantage but proved no match for the competition from US manufacturing giants GAF, Owens-Corning, and others. When these heavy hitters tooled up and began producing their own line of modified bitumen roofing, our client moved to the back of the pack. However, there was one important metric the category killers could not beat: margin. Our client's product line retained the highest percentage profit margin on sales.

It would take massive amounts of capital to scale the company into the top tier, so the founder devised a more affordable exit strategy. His plan was to adapt commercial MB technology and enter the residential roofing market.

Leveraging its existing reputation and technology as a platform, the company set out to launch a premium residential shingle brand. There were two objectives: 1) to would stand out in an overcrowded roofing market and 2) to put a target on the company's back as a prime candidate for acquisition by a much larger competitor.

The Majestic brand emerged ready for prime time and positioned itself as *the world's first industrial-strength roof for the home.*

The Cost of Confusion Methodology was reapplied to the development of core brand elements and high-level messaging all the way down to yard signs, door hangers, and wrappers for every bundle of shingles delivered to the job site.

First-year sales exceeded their initial projections and ttracted a buyer. Just 18 months after Majestic's launch, GAF, the world's largest provider of building materials, acquired the small, innovative Texas manufacturer, delivering a $100 million golden parachute to the company's founder!

ADDITIONAL CASE STUDIES

For additional insight into how the methodology delivers quantifiable results, check out these representative case studies from the archives of Transform Communications.

TECHNOLOGY CASE STUDY

Marketing High-Tech Solutions to Seriously Low-Tech Industries

Impact: Achieving a 267% sales increase over 14 months

Situation: Bar code scanning has revolutionized manual workflows in every industry sector, but it remains a much harder sell to industries relatively untouched by sophisticated technology. Systems Application Engineering (SAE) targeted warehouse distribution centers then running on paper-guided processes. SAE introduced this untapped market to Selector Pro®, the industry's first barcode driven order selection system. Even with its "first-mover advantage," the company posted disappointing initial sales of only $350,000. The sales team reported that prospects just didn't seem to understand how the system worked.

Response: SAE was founded by engineers, so not surprisingly, it's sales materials and conversations focused on the technology features, not on the customer benefits. What was missing was a compelling business case. Through interviews with developers and customers, we zeroed in on the system's dramatic impacts on productivity, order accuracy, customer service, and profit margins. These became the key message set, articulated with a unique spin for each stakeholder in the purchasing decision process.

Execution: Transform outlined an integrated package of marketing, advertising, sales support, and training. Everything was laser focused on customer **business value**. The platform featured information graphics that quickly gave prospects a functional understanding of the technology and how it was used in the warehouse. Digital video captured the system in action, along with testimonials from warehouse employees and operations managers. All media incorporated common themes and branded visual elements to present a unified image across every sales channel.

Results: Within 14 months of its market relaunch, system sales had reached $9.7 million—a 267% increase! The company has since introduced additional system components that Transform rolled out building on the original product marketing platform and leveraged via a revamped website. Combined sales have consistently been in the range of $35 to $40 million a year since the last refresh.

WATER INDUSTRY CASE STUDY

Collaborative Framework & Toolbox for Industrial Water Reuse

Bridging the private / public culture gap with a practical roadmap for shared success

Situation: After a chance opportunity to hear industry panelists discuss the difficulties of implementing water reuse at their facilities, Transform teamed up with RBF Engineering to secure a research grant from the Industrial Watereuse Foundation (IWR). The objective was to create a global online resource for planning and executing successful industrial water reuse projects.

Response: In contrast to using the conventional research reports the foundation was known for, Transform proposed developing a graphically driven resource guide that would provide the first "how-to" roadmap for industrial water reuse projects. The guide would be shared with private companies and public water agencies to better align their respective efforts on behalf of water sustainability. An addendum focused on case studies, technical requirements, and lessons learned.

Execution: Following surveys and interviews with a variety of stakeholders in previously completed projects, Transform pinpointed a set of culture gaps that led to breakdowns in cooperation between private and public sector constituencies. Also identified was an opportunity to "cross-pollinate" knowledge from capital project management by presenting a best-practice project lifecycle process. Centered on a five-phase framework, the guide offered key concepts, business rationale, details on phase activities, milestones, deliverables, decisions, communications, and other required elements for successful delivery of IWR projects.

Results: Since its release, this groundbreaking resource guide has been used worldwide in workshops and webinars to foster more productive collaboration among owners of industrial facilities, public water agencies, regulatory bodies, and municipalities. To jumpstart their efforts, interested parties simply download the publicly available IWR Project Charter template. This tool has helped water providers and their industrial customers to develop and document a comprehensive, shared understanding of each project from the outset. The guide continues to play a role in the ongoing education and outreach of the Industrial Watereuse Foundation, driving a steady, measurable increase in the annual amount of water being recycled by manufacturing and processing plants worldwide.

CORPORATE ACQUISITION CASE STUDY

Refreshing an internal brand expands the technical knowledge base and updates training to onboard thousands of "new" employees coast-to-coast.

Situation: In late 2018, a major U.S. oil refining company completed a $23.3 billion acquisition to become the #1 refiner (by size) in the country. The deal added ten refineries and 30,000 employees west of the Mississippi. The need to standardize the execution of more than $2 billion of capital projects annually would be a critical success factor in delivering the projected return on investment (ROI). Adding to the challenge was the fact that the purchased company had grown through roll-ups of smaller refiners whose processes and project organizations varied significantly, resulting in little consistency from one location to another.

Response: The project management organization used the acquisition as a catalyst to "reboot" the company's long-time project management platform (MPMP). Transform developed the company's original and branded set of application guidelines and tools. And for more than a decade, Transform has continued to expand these resources. The ongoing reboots include not only redesigns but also a demonstration a top-to-bottom recommitment to the disciplined application of the project process companywide.

Execution: Along with developing a new, cleaner "look" to all design elements, Transform also streamlined the amount of information for a "just-in-time" delivery model. Long-form guidelines were redesigned as modular "bytes" accessed via a graphically "reskinned" SharePoint portal and interactive project flow charts. Two high-level overviews focused on internal customers and stakeholders and spelled out their shared responsibilities for success. When all the component parts were completed, Transform scripted and directed production of a four-minute motion graphics video to launch the coast-to-coast introduction of MPMP to the employees of the new acquisition.

Results: Initially, the revamped training modules cut classroom time from five days to three, saving hundreds of thousands of dollars in out-of-office time and travel expenses. When plans for the nationwide roadshow had to be scrapped due to Covid-19, the project management group repurposed all the digital assets to create virtual training courses that veteran employees and their newly-acquired counterparts cited as the most effective training they had ever experienced.

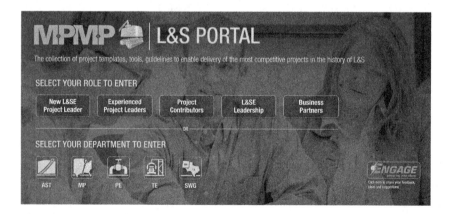

Figure 8.6

Most notable, however, is the dramatic improvement in Marathon's benchmarked project performance. Reducing costs overall by 10% and shortening schedules by 20% enabled the company to move into the top tier of its industry peers. The cost savings alone effectively unlocked $200 million/year from the $2 billion capital budget, enabling the company to expand its capital project portfolio with no increase to its annual budget.

CASE STUDY

Rapid Deployment of a Global Project Management System

Developing, branding, packaging, and rolling out an expert knowledge base to enhance the critical capability

Situation. A large acquisition brought major projects from three continents into the capital project portfolio of a North Carolina-based chemicals company. Each ongoing project was at least ten times larger than any previous project in the company's history, and the firm was committed to ensuring competitive and predictive execution of them all.

Response. Recognizing the critical need to strengthen project management capability worldwide, the company contracted Leading Projects, LLC to develop a project delivery system and online knowledge base. Leading Projects added Transform Communications to its team to handle internal branding, information design, and production of knowledge resources, tools, and training, as well as overall communications. The new project system launched as a strategic initiative to embed major project expertise throughout the organization and get each global project back on track.

Execution. The team recommended a triage approach, focusing on producing high-level frameworks, process maps, knowledge resources, and guidelines to fill in the most critical capability gaps first. To build out the in-depth knowledge base, LP's team of subject matter experts developed draft text in concert with Albemarle counterparts. The signed-off drafts flowed to Transform for major editing and development of information graphics. Upon final approval, Transform produced APP branded deliverables in a wide range of formats, including print, eDocs, video, computer learning, etc.

The initial set of deliverables rolled out in just six months and was put to work immediately through workshops in the U.S., Chile, China, and Australia. Milestones at 12 and 18 months brought additional topics and tools into the knowledge library. By the end of the assignment, Leading Projects' technical SMEs and Transform's information design team had delivered a fully integrated system of communications, know-ledge resources, and actionable job aids for access via an online portal with a branded user interface. (See deliverables next page.)

Results: Early interventions by the APP team surfaced key project issues and quickly provided some early "wins." Major project teams soon aligned their efforts to the new framework and began to make course corrections. As the process was rolled out to legacy sites, the reaction was overwhelmingly positive. The consensus among users was, "Hmm, this looks very different from previous corporate efforts." Engagement with the portal and its resources has exceeded expectations, with more than 1000 registered users adding 1000 projects. At the board level, the company expressed its confidence in the ability of the engineering organization to handle the major projects portfolio. Albemarle's APP project lead noted that the new communications and training received high compliments for being more polished and impactful than those of the substantially larger SAP initiative that had been conducted previously by a leading global consulting firm.

Focusing on workforce engagement, Leading Projects and Transform deployed a project management system that enabled the client to steer its portfolio of global projects back on track while closing the gap on massive cost overruns and delays.

Chapter 9

From Engineer to Change Agent

"Why should you take my word for it?"

That's the question I asked myself that inspired this addition to the book. I'm like everyone else who writes leadership and management books like this one. We purport to be experts, laying out our theories and offering our opinions as if they were gospel truth.

I know this stuff works, so why not talk to someone else who knows that, too? I thought it would be great to wrap up the book with a client's perspective. That someone is Jeff Heath, PE, PMP (Professional Engineer and Project Management Professional). Jeff spent the last 20 years of his career transforming project management inside a major U.S. refining company.

I was fortunate to meet Jeff soon after launching Transform Communications. He "got it"—that is, he understood the Cost of Confusion and became a treasured client champion. When I approached him about the idea of a conversation for the book, he was all in. I hope our conversation provides readers with some practical takeaways.

Rich What was going on in your organization that led to our working together?

Jeff I was in an engineering and capital project group trying to understand why we had such wildly inconsistent project performance. Some projects were solid successes, while others were astounding failures, to the tune of several hundred million dollars. It came down to the fact that execution was based on the individual experience of the project leader. There was no process. There was no rhyme or reason to anything that anybody did, so the results couldn't be anything but inconsistent. It always came down to the capability or natural instincts of the person managing the project.

The only way to address this was to establish a proven framework and practices that insulates the project from the damage an inexperienced or bad project manager could cause. Our

DOI: 10.4324/9781003301080-9

industry competitors (as well as other industries) were creating disciplined, consistent processes for managing and executing projects. These companies communicated clearly and concisely, they presented the rationale, explained the value, and measured their results. We had some catching up to do.

Rich   What was your reaction the first time I explained the Cost of Confusion to you?

Jeff   It just made so much sense. We had been through so many initiatives that started and then fizzled out. It felt like there was no real plan, no follow on with any kind of consistent communication, a consistent message about what something was, why it mattered, and how to execute on it was often lacking.

The improvement initiatives all kind of blurred together, like, "OK, this is what's coming out this month," and that's the first and last time anybody heard about it. There wasn't much thought given to their lifecycle, ultimate adoption, and internalization.

So, this (the Cost of Confusion) made a lot of sense to me.

Rich   I used to joke that that the typical communications plan for a corporate initiative was taking a logo a team member designed in PowerPoint and getting it printed on coffee mugs and notebooks. If it was a really big deal, there would be logos on shirts and "gimme" caps. The teams handed out this stuff as if was supposed to part the waters for everyone and bring everyone to the promised land. Of course, it never worked like that.

Jeff   We started by putting together a do-it-yourself one-pager. Do you remember the horrible set of icons for the five-phase project process I showed you?

Rich   Oh, yeah.

Jeff   The first process phase was a collection of geometric shapes, then a phase symbolized by a triangle, and it ended up with the final phase being represented by a pyramid with a camel and a palm tree. Probably done in PowerPoint. I mean, that's what we would have been stuck with while we tried to get people interested. There was nothing compelling in the least.

Rich   e talked about what level of design quality and production value it would take to launch this initiative with impact. How difficult was it to convince people to let you bring somebody in to help?

Jeff   You know, people recognized that we had a problem with projects. They saw this initiative as something that we needed to invest in. So, it wasn't hard to get past the idea. It was more just, OK, how do we communicate this in the right way?

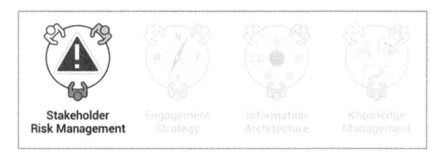

Figure 9.1

How We Applied the Methodology

Rich I think that's a universal challenge for anyone who has a great idea they want to see implemented. It's going to come down to how well they can communicate it to decision-makers.

Jeff Exactly, exactly. I think after we met, that was one of the first things that we talked about. Who are the stakeholders who are going to make this go forward? Who can stop this?

Rich I didn't have a name for it at the time, but in the methodology, it became stakeholder risk assessment—identifying that core group of stakeholders up and down the organizational ladder. We had to figure out who could shut it down.

Jeff Initially, I wrote the classic double-spaced memo. This is what we think we need to do. Other companies have done it. How do we how do we learn from their mistakes? Here are the people that helped them do it. How do we take all this and turn it into something that we can use to save a lot of money on our capital development projects and reduce the risk of project failure?

  I got the vice president of the engineering & technology group to help me with the letter, because he got it right away. It was the level above him that really was the most challenging because they had new initiatives and employee programs pitched by multiple organizations weekly.

  So, you really had to differentiate yourself. How do you get their attention and keep it long enough to get a yes or no? Or worse, they not only don't do this, but they don't come back to my office. Fortunately, I had that first high-level brochure that laid out the proposed business process across two pages with color icons and captions., laying out the problem, why it mattered, and the powerful, concise solution. They had never seen anything like it before.

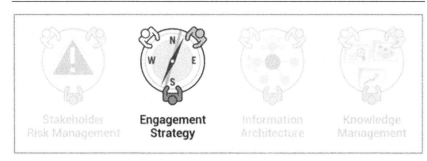

Stakeholder Risk Management   **Engagement Strategy**   Information Architecture   Knowledge Management

Figure 9.2

Rich	After that clearing that first hurdle, we had to figure out all the messaging, that is, what each stakeholder group needed to hear to green-light the idea and let it go forward.
Jeff	Exactly! At the level where you're talking to the project manager, you have one message: how do we make your life easier? How do we reduce your career risk? How do we make you and your projects successful? Then, as you move up the chain, it becomes a different message. We had to hit executive hot buttons like making capital projects more predictable and profitable, improving ROCE, Return On Capital Employed leading to improved "**EBITDA**, earnings before interest, taxes, depreciation, and amortization, and probably most importantly, how do we eliminate large project disasters? They're completely different messages.
Rich	I think that's a subtle point not well understood by teams leading initiatives. You can't just promote one dimension. People all have different reasons for buying in.
Jeff	It was curious, my immediate supervisors were sort of agnostic to a project management process initially. I don't know if it was because they had other priorities they were working on and didn't really have the bandwidth or they were afraid of getting their name associated with another failed initiative. They just weren't very interested until after this senior VP got it.
	He oversaw an operating organization that had the budget to execute large capital projects, so he was someone who could make it happen or keep it from happening. Fortunately, he was one of the big proponents. Suddenly, everyone wanted to get on board.
Rich	We convinced him to do a video interview with me. I asked the question, "So what's the value of this?"

Jeff   His answer was: "The thing I love about this is I don't care where you apply it—it could be a small operating group; it could be in any large functional organization across this company; you can apply this process and do nothing but make money."

And it was just such a great off-the-cuff answer. You know he got it. He understood it. And once he made that remark, everything kind of took off. It was kind of a tipping point for this whole thing. Getting senior VP endorsement and then having another executive say, "I'm not looking at any project that doesn't have a Decision Support Package"(a cornerstone of the project management process)—those guys communicated a very clear, concise, easy to understand message that left no room for opting out of the process.

Rich   When people started to see the communications roll out and bubble up in the organization, what was the impact of that? When did you recognize that we had momentum?

Jeff   Well, it kind of went from, "OK, you guys have talked about this, but I guess we're really doing this."

After sending out that first brochure that explained the process, we could have said, "Well, good luck with what you're trying to do." Instead, we followed that with an overall communications program. There were regular communications and meetings with supervisors and managers and project leaders. We had this process that had been fully documented, the brochures, the pocket cards, the videos, and all kinds of tools. There were wall charts and guidelines, and everything had an orchestrated, consistent look and feel, consistent messaging and common terminology.

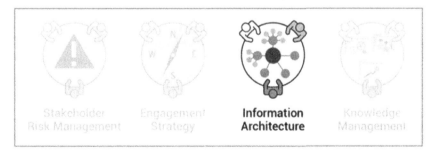

Stakeholder   Engagement   **Information**   Knowledge
Risk Management   Strategy   **Architecture**   Management

Figure 9.3

We brought it together and delivered two-day training courses to all project managers and supervisors at all our sites. After people left that training, they realized, "I can either walk away from any more of this and hope that it goes away, or I can get on board. I would say probably two-thirds got onboard right away. It took the others a little bit longer, but eventually, everyone was applying the process to their projects and using the tools. People adopted the process, and it continued to evolve over the next ten years.

Bumps in the Road

Rich   Sometimes it's the organization itself that prevents us from adding the value we know is there. How many times did you have a supportive boss yanked out your department and replaced with someone who had no understanding of what you guys had accomplished? It was like being sent back to square one to educate the person that you were reporting and justify your existence all over again.

Jeff   Yes, I came to see this as part of the territory. Fortunately, it helped having a tight story and all the communication tools you created to provide a clear path to understanding. We accepted it was going to happen again and again, so we prepared for it.

We were able to walk into anybody's office and show them this compendium of information, all its layers, and how it tracks so well from the highest-level description all the way through all the documentation to the web presence. Everything was clear and clean, smooth and easy to follow. And we did that more than once. We would walk into a new refinery manager's office and say, I know you may be familiar with this but let us show you how it flows and why we need two days of your people's time to review this process or to go through an updated training course.

And now it's made it so much easier than relying on relationships and hand waving for attention. That's how you get through the door with the gatekeepers. It was these materials they just can't argue with or deny because it's so well crafted.

Gaining Visibility

Rich   What did it mean for you? How did it impact you over the course of your career, being the guy that brought this kind of stuff to the table?

Jeff   Well, what instantly happened was we got to design a department and my job. We went from there was no such thing as an Office of Project Management to a department in which I got to define what we needed to do to support the project leaders and project teams being asked to apply this powerful business process. And a lot of that had to do with my being the face and the voice of this thing across the entire company. I didn't understand the benefit of that at the time, but ultimately it paid big dividends down the road. I say down the road, because you may remember the organization I was in was blown up—and I helped. I was facilitating a reengineering team that was looking at outsourcing the project and engineering department I was in. I didn't put it together at first, but one day I realized that they're going to outsource my job.

Rich   And you're helping them!

Jeff   Yes, that was tough, but the connections and visibility I gained through rolling out and then supporting the business segments projects enabled me to jump to another business segment to lay the project management process gospel down and embed it in the way they did business—whereas many of my contemporaries at the time left the corporation.

Visual Problem Solving

Rich   Many people don't realize how important visualization has become and how powerful it is when done artfully. What was the impact on your organization?

Jeff   Sitting down to visualize the conceptual and philosophical things we were discussing—that was new to us.

Rich   I always preach that PowerPoint-free communications give you a huge advantage. In your case, you got to have an exclusive visual platform and toolbox to operate with all these years.

Jeff   It was the easiest thing because I got to the place where I had so many visual elements from you that I could produce about

Figure 9.4

anything that I needed. Rough enough for whatever it was I needed on that day, and then, when I had the time, I could come back to you and pull it into whatever current design version we were in.

Rich   Well, I would always look forward to our mind-meld conversations about visuals. You'd say, "I'm trying to accomplish this and communicate this." Then, we would sit and sketch on our respective virtual napkins. I would take a photo and text my idea over the fence at you. Then you threw it back over the fence at me. That would go on until we had the right elements logically arranged in a PowerPoint slide. I would send the slide to my design partners to work their magic. Eventually, I stopped referring to them as graphic designers and started calling them "visual problem solvers."

Jeff   I don't know how you guys do this, to go from chicken scratch ideas for a graphic and end up with something that tells the story and maintains an overall look and feel.

Rich   There is something rewarding about conveying a complex technical concept through a series of images. Maybe it's a road map; maybe it's a layered cutaway, maybe it's a color-coded illustration. Unfortunately, the notion of visual thinking is one that designers working in corporate graphic services departments don't have the luxury of providing. You know, they're sort of treated as order takers.

Jeff   Right— in fairness to them, that's not what they're asked to do 90% of the time. It's what you just described—drop a picture here, put an illustration there. They're not asked to do much more than that. So, the few times that I went to our internal graphics department to talk to someone and explain what I was trying to do, I got exactly what I asked for. It wasn't a situation in which the person could think differently about it or think better about it.

Delivering Value to the Organization

Rich   I always felt like I was selling to an unrecognized need, so I learned to start defining it in terms of loss avoidance. "What's it gonna cost you if this thing fails? If there is $1,000,000 or more at risk, what's the problem with finding $50,000 or even $100,000 for us to build the polished professional communications platform and tools you need to get you where you want to go?"

Jeff   No, I mean, that's exactly right. In most cases, we were able to find money to get things done. It didn't line up perfectly with when we needed it. Or maybe it wasn't exactly the amount, but you and your team always delivered something to help us raise the bar.

Some of the smaller things got us great visibility, like the pocket cards and wall charts. We would see our wall posters up in every coffee bar in every refinery that we visited.

That stuff was really powerful. It lent this credibility to everything that we did. And it blew away the stuff that other people (firms) we brought in would try to do.

Rich   I've referred to you for years as Transform's biggest client champion—somebody who recognized the value we delivered. I think about the times that I'd get a call from you to tell me about an initiative in another organization. You sensed these people were about to end up in the ditch. You'd say," I'm gonna introduce you. Just help them and charge it to my budget."

Jeff   Yeah, we had so many times when a group had a great idea. They just didn't have a way to kind of get it from where they were at to where they needed to go, so, I would parachute you in.

The One that Got Away

Rich   There was one opportunity that got away, though.

Jeff   That's right! The capital project budget process was broken. Each year, we talked about it and would look back at how many projects people sweat blood over that never got implemented. Some years it was 50% of those proposed. That meant a huge number of hours put into front-end budgeting work was a complete waste of effort. We're talking thousands of man-hours tied up in creating numbers that didn't mean anything. Absolutely nothing.

There were three or four of us that worked on it part-time, one of those midnight to 2:00 AM kind of things. At one point, we did get it in front of the senior VP Finance and the CEO. They both loved it, but we could never make the leap to get the resources and time it was going to need to take off.

What About Impact?

Rich   Looking back on time in the trenches and at the work that we've done together, what stands out as the thing that made the biggest big impact?

Jeff   You know, it's funny because it took me a long time to think about it in meaningful terms.

The organization had reached the point where it started benchmarking every project over $10 million. A project industry benchmarking and research group, IPA (Independent Project Analysis), with a huge database of projects, would come in, look at each one of our projects and compare it to their database. They would tell you many things about your project practices, and it's ultimate performance, including whether your cost was within the industry average, above it, or below it.

We had metrics on projects completed before the new project management process was introduced and metrics on projects that were managed with the process. IPA found the difference in those two groups was somewhere between 18 and 20%.

At the time, 18 to 20% of the annual capital budget came to over $200 million. So, over the five or six or seven years I was promoting the process everywhere I could, the company saved over $800 million.

So that's the impact from a dollar perspective. There was nothing else in this company that had shown anything close to that kind of improvement in performance anywhere.

Also, for me, as important as the implementation of this project process, and getting it to stick was reducing the stress in individual project leader's lives and reducing the career risk associated with delivering a "bad" project.

Rich   And that's not a one-off number because the organization hasn't stopped doing projects, and now the process is completely embedded in how every project is executed.

Jeff   In terms of impact, there is also a cultural perspective. Historically, it was all fear based. Leadership expected project teams to do things on a shoestring, and keep projects as low cost as possible. But then, as soon as they failed to meet these completely unreasonable demands, project managers got called on the carpet and blasted:

"I'll have your head on a plate by the end of the day! You're not going to go anywhere in this company!"

Project teams didn't trust the leadership team. The leadership team didn't trust project teams. And nobody trusted the numbers.

As a result of this work, a lot of the fear was driven out of the system by holding everyone accountable for the process.

We built a new level of communication and trust between the business and project teams leading to much more competitive projects.

Crossed Paths and Surprising Directions

Jeff   We've moved into our new house, so I'm emptying out boxes and found a stack of stuff we had done. It got me thinking about my career path if we had not met. I'm sure I would have been let go in the first downsizing wave. If not, then I would have left at some point because just doing construction or IT projects, did not fuel me. I realized creating large corporate change that improves peoples' work life while driving large bottom-line benefits is my path of choice.

So, the very fact that we created this core critical mass that took on a life of its own permeated the culture of the company, and became a language across the company—gave me the ability to basically float in and out of every operating organization's project group that I wanted. I could move from one organization to another, do the same optimization there, and move back.

That's not the kind of freedom most corporations will let you have, to say I want to go someplace else but be able to come back. I know that none of it would have happened if we hadn't crossed paths and you had not taught me the ways of a "Communications Jedi".

Rich   I appreciate that, Jeff. Had we not crossed paths, we wouldn't be having this conversation, and there would be no book for people to read. I have learned so much from working with you and steeping in all the project management knowledge there was to convey.

Jeff   I used to tell people that you could translate engineer-speak into something fit for human consumption. You're one of those people with the ability to translate for the rest of the organization.

Rich   When I would describe you to people over the years, I would say, "This is a guy who can walk into an executive meeting, ask the right questions and save the company $2,000,000. And he does it on a weekly basis,"

Jeff   I read a great quote once: "Project management is the crucible in which great careers are forged."

It certainly forged mine. I learned that communication is critical to making any of this stuff (projects) happen. You can have the greatest idea in the world but if you can't communicate it effectively, succinctly, in terms that people can grasp, and make it fit into this bigger picture of where we're trying to go—it doesn't matter what your idea is.

In Celebration of Change Agents

Rich   A friend of mine asked me who this book was for, and I thought of the broad audience that reads business books. But I realized, I wrote it for people like you—change agents. They look around their organizations and see all the potential that's not being realized, the talent that's underused, the effort that is needlessly wasted—and they want to make a difference. So, the book outfits them with a new lens through which to view the workplace. Then, it lays out a methodology and toolset that I hope empowers readers to have the kind of impact that you have had.

Jeff   If you really know what your value is, communicate it to those around and above you; you can land on your feet regardless of how stable or unstable the work environment you're in. Continuing to do the things that you like to do—that has been the key for me. I loved every minute!

Oh, some of my bosses were better than others, as were some of the organizations. But the work was always there, it was always interesting, and I got to work with very, very dedicated people who really wanted to make things happen. There was a lot of fun, I have no regrets.

Rich   Jeff, I can't thank you enough for such an inspired way to wrap up this book. We set out to change your organization, but that experience changed you, your career path, and the impact that you have had on the entire company.

Resources

Cost of Confusion Certified

Transform Communications

Information design and strategic communications
https://www.transformcom.com

Gotham Image Works, A Hart Energy Company

Producers of video, 3D animation, and events
https://gothamimageworks.com

times2studios

Visual thinkers in branding, design, and information graphics
https://times2studio.com

PRIME, Inc.

Experts in website development and digital marketing
https://prime-incorporated.com

Leading Projects, LLC

Innovators in project management systems, capability, and performance
https://leading-projects.com

Online

Edward Tufte.com

Tufte is the "father of data visualization" whose knowledge is foundational to cutting the cost of confusion. His courses, books, and tools are essential learning for information designers.

URL: HTTPS://WWW.EDWARDTUFTE.COM/TUFTE/

VISUAL CAPITALIST.COM

Online showcase for the information design community that explores business, financial and economic concepts, wide ranging styles, and topics for inspiration and trends in visualization
URL: HTTPS://WWW.VISUALCAPITALIST.COM

Blog: *Remote Work: Lessons learned building the workplace of the future*
URL: HTTPS://BLOG.DOIST.COM/CATEGORY/REMOTE-WORK/

An online platform dedicated to sharing best practices, highlighting emerging ideas, and offering moral support to remote workers worldwide.

READING

TITLE: *Unstuck: A Tool for Yourself, Your Team, and Your World*

AUTHORS: Keith Yamashita and Sandra Spataro

PUBLISHER: Penguin Putnam Trade (April 2004)

Introduces the "Serious Seven" states of stuck that can mire individuals, teams, and organizations, and offers solutions for getting out them and moving forward toward success

1. Overwhelmed
2. Exhausted
3. Directionless
4. Hopeless
5. Battle-Torn
6. Worthless
7. Alone

TITLE: *Visual Thinking: The Hidden Gifts of People Who Think in Pictures, Patterns, and Abstractions*

AUTHOR: Temple Grandin, Ph.D.

PUBLISHER: Riverhead Books (October 2022)
Bringing a new dimension to diversity, Temple Grandin makes us understand how a world increasingly geared to the verbal tends to sideline visual thinkers, screening them out at school and passing over them in the workplace. Rather than continuing to waste their singular gifts, driving a collective loss in productivity and innovation, Grandin proposes new approaches to educating, parenting, employing, and collaborating with visual thinkers. In a highly competitive world, this important book helps us see, we need every mind on board.

TITLE: *Deep Work: Rules for Focused Success in a Distracted World*

AUTHOR: Cal Newport

PUBLISHER: Grand Central Publishing (January 2016)

Newport, a computer science professor, offers insight on how professionals can and must make an impact when their work is a frantic blur of e-mail, instant messaging, and online collaboration. His framework of four rules empowers readers to cultivate deep work skills that will produce

TITLE: *The Power of Clarity: Unleash the True Potential of Workplace Productivity, Confidence, and Empowerment*

AUTHOR: Ann Latham

PUBLISHER: Bloomsbury Publishing (July 2021)

Consultant Ann Latham springboards off a Fortune 500 study that found as much as 80% of working time is lost to tiresome meetings, unclear expectations, difficult decisions, and other wasteful delays. Leveraging her in-depth experience, the author guides leaders in focusing on clarity to increase workplace productivity and effectiveness. The value proposition is how to deliver better results in far less time while also increasing confidence and commitment.

TITLE: *The Catalyst: How to Change Anyone's Mind*

AUTHOR: Jonah Berger

PUBLISHER: Simon & Schuster UK (March 2020)

This book offers fresh thinking on the nature of change by recasting change agents as catalysts. Instead of asking, "How could I change someone's mind?" catalysts ask a different question: "Why haven't they changed already? What's stopping them?" Catalysts focus on removing roadblocks and reducing the barriers to change.

Berger takes an in-depth look at how catalysts can be effective in the toughest of situations: how hostage negotiators get people to come out with their hands up, how marketers get new products to catch on, how leaders transform organizational culture, how activists ignite social movements, how substance abuse counselors get addicts to realize they have a problem, and how political campaigners change deeply rooted political beliefs.

TITLE: *Simple: Conquering the Crisis of Complexity*

AUTHORS: Alan Siegel and Irene Etzkorn

PUBLISHER: Grand Central Publishing (April 2013)

Simple is the culmination of the authors' work together consulting with businesses and organizations around the world to streamline products, services, processes, and communications. The book illustrates the dramatic benefits that can be achieved through having empathy, striving for clarity, and distilling a compelling message. The results combine to reduce the distance between company and customer, hospital and patient, government and citizen.

Examining the best and worst practices of an array of organizations big and small, including the IRS, Google, Philips, Trader Joe's, Chubb Insurance, and ING Direct, and many more, the authors recast simplicity as a mindset, a design aesthetic, and a writing technique.

TITLE: *Change the Culture, Change the Game: The Breakthrough Strategy for Energizing Your Organization and Creating Accountability for Results**

AUTHORS: Roger Connors and Tom Smith

PUBLISHER: Penguin Random House (June 2012)

Groundbreaking work that explores the critical role of culture and offers a practical strategy for leaders to implement a culture change, energize their organizations, and create greater accountability for results. This book addresses creation of a set of cultural beliefs and introduces "The Results Pyramid," a model to clarify what matters and establish accountability for it, and leaders accelerate culture change.

TITLE: *Leading Change*

AUTHOR: John Kotter

PUBLISHER: Harvard Business Review (November 2012)

John Kotter's now-legendary eight-step process for managing change with positive results has become the foundation for leaders and organizations across the globe. By outlining the process every organization must go through to achieve its goals and by identifying where and how even top performers derail during the change process, Kotter provides a practical resource for leaders and managers charged with making change initiatives work. Leading Change is widely recognized as his seminal work and is an important precursor to his newer ideas on acceleration published in Harvard Business Review.

TITLE: *Managing Complexity in Global Organizations*

AUTHORS: Ulrich Steger, Wolfgang Amann, and Martha L. Maznevski

PUBLISHER: Wiley (May 2007)

SYNOPSIS: Corporate decision-making is more challenging than ever before owing to the diversity of cultures, customers, competitors, and regulations. In an effort to understand these dynamics, the authors draw from their academic research to identify four key drivers of complexity (diversity; interdependence; ambiguity, and flux), and then they outline solutions on specific issues in a variety of functions, industries, and markets.

TITLE: *The Laws of Simplicity*

AUTHOR: John Maeda

PUBLISHER: MIT Press (July 2006)

Responding to the proliferation of digital communication, consumer electronics, global media platforms and information channels, the author offers ten laws for balancing simplicity and complexity in business, technology, and design. These rules provide guiding principles for business leaders, entrepreneurs, product engineers, and other professional disciplines. Maeda's concise guide to simplicity in the digital age shows us how this idea can be a cornerstone of organizations and their products—how it can drive both business and technology.

TITLE: *Don't Think of an Elephant! Know Your Values and Frame the Debate**

AUTHOR: George Lakoff

PUBLISHER: Chelsea Green Publishing Company (September 2004)

This work describes political framing and analyzes the ways in which it is being used to sway and manipulate public opinion, determine voting patterns, and even change people's political orientation. Lakoff's years of research and work with leading activists and policymakers have been distilled into this essential guide, which shows progressives how to think in terms of values instead of programs, and why people support policies which align with their values and identities, even when running counter to their best interests.

TITLE: *The Tipping Point: How Little Things Can Make a Big Difference**

AUTHOR: Malcolm Gladwell

PUBLISHER: Little, Brown and Company (January 2000)

Gladwell's breakthrough notion theorized three variables that determine whether and when a product, idea, or phenomenon will reach a "tipping point" that launches it into widespread adoption / impact – aka "going viral." Understanding this previously undiscovered dynamic equipped his audience with a strategic framework to increase the probability of runaway success.

TITLE: *Information Anxiety*

AUTHOR: Richard Saul Wurman

PUBLISHER: Doubleday (January 1989)

Wurman identifies a special ailment of this age of communications caused by an overwhelming flood of data from all corners of society. The author, a graphic artist, and architect, argues that "learning is remembering what you are interested in," and proposes the ongoing need for organizations to transform information into structured knowledge. Also included are specific information-processing skills and media habits to help people manage their limited bandwidth.

Bibliography

Chapter 2: Confusing Customers

1. Hunsberger, Brent. "Faltering in the wake of marketing and service missteps." *The Oregonian*, (Portland, OR), Jan. 6, 2008, p. D03.
2. Hosier, Lewis. Owner of Wired World Technologies, in discussion with the author, Jan. 2021.
3. Hamilton, David P. "Despite Cutting-Edge Technology, 'PVRs' Prove to Be a Difficult Sell." *The Wall Street Journal*, Feb. 7, 2001. https://www.wsj.com/articles/SB981503494826920845.
4. Lawton, Christopher. "The War on Returns." *The Wall Street Journal*, May 8, 2008. 2008.https://www.wsj.com/articles/SB121020824820975641.
5. PYMNTS, Staff. "65% of Consumer Electronics Returns Occur During Setup." Pymnts.com (publisher, What's Next Media & Analytics), September 7, 2021. https://www.pymnts.com/news/retail/2021/most-consumer-electronics-returns-occur-during-setup/.
6. Landro, Laura. "Tips to Better Understand Those Doctor's Orders." *The Wall Street Journal*, July 3, 2003. https://www.wsj.com/articles/SB105718151940549300.
7. Landro, Laura. "Hospitals Combat Errors at the 'Hand-Off'." *The Wall Street Journal*, June 28, 2006. https://www.wsj.com/articles/SB115145533775992541.
8. Institute for Healthcare Improvement. "SBAR: Situation-Background-Assessment-Recommendation." IHI.org, accessed Dec. 12, 2021. https://www.ihi.org/Topics/SBARCommunicationTechnique/Pages/default.aspx.
9. National Academy of Medicine. "Medication Errors Injure 1.5 Million People and Cost Billions of Dollars Annually; Report Offers Comprehensive Strategies for Reducing Drug-Related Mistakes." National Acadamies.org, July 20, 2006, accessed Dec. 13, 2021. https://www.nationalacademies.org/news/2006/07/medication-errors-injure-one-point-five-million-people-and-cost-billions-of-dollars-annually-report-offers-comprehensive-strategies-for-reducing-drug-related-mistakes.
10. Fortune Business Insights. "Dietary Supplements Market Size, Share & C OVID-19 Impact Analysis." Fortune Business Insights.com, Jan. 2022,

accessed Dec. 17, 2022. https://www.fortunebusinessinsights.com/dietary-supplements-market-102082.

11. Centers for Medicare & Medicaid Services. "National Health Expenditure Data, Historical." CMS.gov, Dec. 15, 2022, accessed Jan. 12, 2023. https://www.cms.gov/research-statistics-data-and-systems/statistics-trends-and-reports/nationalhealthexpenddata/nationalhealthaccountshistorical.

Chapter 3: Confusing Employees

12. DePillis, Lydia. "Why Volkswagen is helping a union organize its own plant." *The Washington Post*, Feb. 10, 2014. https://www.washingtonpost.com/news/wonk/wp/2014/02/10/why-volkswagen-is-helping-a-union-organize-its-own-plant/.

13. Caulkin, Simon. "WL Gore: the company others try and fail to imitate." *Financial Times*, Aug. 1, 2019. https://www.ft.com/content/aee67fe0-ac63-11e9-b3e2-4fdf846f48f5.

14. Tam, Pui-Wing. "The Corporate Strategist." *Wall Street Journal*, May 13. 2002. https://www.wsj.com/articles/SB1020883126101560400.

15. Marchese, David. "The Digital Workplace Is Designed to Bring You Down." *New York Times Magazine*, Jan. 22, 2023. https://www.nytimes.com/interactive/2023/01/23/magazine/cal-newport-interview.html.

16. Weber, Lauren. "Company's Trick to Getting 95,000 Hours Back? Canceling Meetings." *Wall Street Journal*, Feb. 1. 2023. https://www.wsj.com/articles/bosses-reduce-meetings-employee-productivity-11675263710.

17. Latham, Ann. *The Power of Clarity: Unleash the True Potential of Workplace Productivity, Confidence, and Empowerment*. Bloomsbury Publishing, 2021.

Chapter 4: Confusing Citizens

18. Fuhrmans, Vanessa. "Health Savings Plans Start to Falter." *Wall Street Journal*, June 12, 2007. https://www.wsj.com/articles/SB118161312384432069.

19. Devenir Newsroom. "2021 Devenir & HSA Council Demographic Survey Findings." Devenir.com, July 11, 2022. https://www.devenir.com/2021-devenir-hsa-council-demographic-survey-findings/.

20. Prater, Erin. "Meet the biology professor who named the surging 'Kraken' COVID variant. He has more to help make sense of Omicron's 'alphabet soup.'" Fortune Well.com, Jan. 5, 2023. https://fortune.com/well/2023/01/05/kraken-variant-omicron-covid-name-ryan-gregory-biology-professor/.

21. DeSilver, Drew. "Turnout in U.S. has soared in recent elections but by some measures still trails that of many other countries." Pew Research Centers, Nov. 1, 2022. https://www.pewresearch.org/short-reads/2022/11/01/turnout-in-u-s-has-soared-in-recent-elections-but-by-some-measures-still-trails-that-of-many-other-countries/.

22. Lee, Suevon. "Five of the Most Confusing Ballots in the Country." ProPublica.org, Nov. 5, 2012. https://www.propublica.org/article/five-of-the-most-confusing-ballots-in-the-country.

23. Lakoff, George. *The All-New Don't Think Of An Elephant!: Know Your Values And Frame The Debate.* Chelsea Green Publishing, 2014.

24. Jones, Bradley. "Increasing share of Americans favor a single government program to provide health care coverage." Pew Research Centers, Sept. 29, 2020. https://www.pewresearch.org/short-reads/2020/09/29/increasing-share-of-americans-favor-a-single-government-program-to-provide-health-care-coverage/#:~:text=A%2054%25%20majority%20of%20Democrats,up%20from%2044%25%20last%20year.

25. Centers for Medicare and Medicaid Services (CMS). "Hospital Price Transparency.) CMS.gov, page accessed Feb. 9, 2023. https://www.cms.gov/hospital-price-transparency.

26. Keisler-Starkey, Katherine and Bunch, Lisa N." Health Insurance Coverage in the United States: 2021." United States Census Bureau, Sept. 13, 2022. https://www.census.gov/library/publications/2022/demo/p60-278.html.

27. Raghavan, Anita, Kranhold, Kathryn and Barrionuevo, Alexei. "How Enron Bosses Created A Culture of Pushing Limits." *Wall Street Journal*, Aug. 26, 2002. https://www.wsj.com/articles/SB1030320285540885115.

28. Hays, Kristen. "Enron on Brink of Bankruptcy." *Associated Press*, Nov. 29, 2001. Viewed on Corpwatch.org, Oct. 4, 2022. https://www.corpwatch.org/article/usa-enron-brink-bankruptcy.

29. Powell, Jamie. "Enron: blast from the past [update]." *Financial Times*, Feb. 13, 2020. https://www.ft.com/content/80a6ee52-98ee-4ccc-8183-a68968c5fc9a.

Chapter 6: Deadly Confusion

30. Schleifstein, Mark. "How many people died in Hurricane Katrina? Toll reduced 17 years later." *Times-Picayune* (New Orleans, LA), Jan 14, 2023. https://www.nola.com/news/hurricane/how-many-people-died-in-katrina-toll-reduced-17-years-on/article_e3009e46-91ed-11ed-8f2a-a7b11e1e8d34.html.

31. Staff, Texas Tribune. "Five takeaways from the House committee report on the Uvalde shooting." *Texas Tribune*, July 17, 2022. https://www.texastribune.org/2022/07/17/house-uvalde-investigation-takeaways/.

32. Bertorelli, Paul. "Lion Air: Faulty Design, Weak Pilot Training and Maintenance Lapses Caused 737 MAX Crash." Aviation News, Oct. 25, 2019. https://www.avweb.com/aviation-news/lion-air-faulty-design-weak-pilot-training-and-poor-maintenance-caused-737-max-crash/.

33. Topham, Gwyn. "Ethiopian flight 302: second new Boeing 737 to crash in four months." *The Guardian*, Mar. 10, 2019. https://www.theguardian.com/world/2019/mar/10/ethiopian-flight-302-second-new-boeing-737-max-8-to-crash-in-four-months.

34. Gates, Dominic and Baker, Mike. "The inside story of MCAS: How Boeing's 737 MAX system gained power and lost safeguards." *Seattle Times*, June 22, 2019. https://www.seattletimes.com/seattle-news/times-watchdog/the-inside-story-of-mcas-how-boeings-737-max-system-gained-power-and-lost-safeguards/.

35. Gollom, Mark, Shprintsen, Alex, and Zalac, Frédéric. "737 Max flight manual may have left MCAS information on 'cutting room floor.'" Canadian Broadcasting Corporation (CBC), Mar. 26, 2019. https://www.cbc.ca/news/business/boeing-737-manual-mcas-system-plane-crash-1.5065842.

36. National Highway Traffic Safety Administration. "Newly Released Estimates Show Traffic Fatalities Reached a 16-Year High in 2021." NHTSA.gov, May 17, 2022. https://www.nhtsa.gov/press-releases/early-estimate-2021-traffic-fatalities.

37. U.S. Consumer Products Safety Commission. "Kids II Recalls All Rocking Sleepers Due to Reports of Deaths." CPSC.gov, Apr. 26, 2019. https://www.cpsc.gov/Recalls/2019/Kids-II-Recalls-All-Rocking-Sleepers-Due-to-Reports-of-Deaths.

About the Author

Richard A. Layton
CCO | Chief Clarity Officer
Transform Communications

Richard (Rich) Layton is a results-focused, strategic thought leader and originator of the concept, *the Cost of Confusion*.

Boasting the checkered resume of a Renaissance communicator, Rich has been a writer, video producer, factory worker, photographer, rock and roll musician, creative director, marketing director, and production company vice president.

Rich founded Transform Communications in 1992 in Houston, Texas, working in concert with leading consulting firms (e.g., CSC Index, DiBianca Berkman, Deloitte & Touche, et al.) and with direct clients to ensure the success of major organizational change and enterprise technology initiatives.

Prior to establishing Transform, Rich was vice president and creative director for Lunar Productions in Memphis, Tennessee, where he was involved in brand-building and advertising for such notable brands as Federal Express, Holiday Inns, Embassy Suites, ITT, Trustworthy Hardware, and Wyndham Hotels.

Rich's "secret sauce" is a disciplined methodology that blends strategic communications with risk management, helping organizations to identify and overcome complex business, technology, and marketing challenges. The results have delivered, literally, millions of dollars in bottom-line benefits. Engagements have included global project management systems, Corporate Social Responsibility (CSR), SAP implementation, Value/Supply Chain Management, and other critical integration efforts for clients such as Albermarle Lithium, BP, GAF, Marathon Petroleum, Sainsbury's Grocers (UK), Schnitzer Steel and Tesla.

Recognition for Richard's work includes awards from the International Association of Business Communicators (IABC), Society for Technical Communications, International Telly Awards, Houston International Film Festival, and the Blue-Chip Enterprise Award. His articles, editorials, and white papers have appeared in professional publications, on websites, and course reading lists around the world. Richard also has been a keynote presenter and workshop leader in a variety of forums, including the Center for Information-Development Management, the Software Association of Oregon, Portland State University (MBA program), HR Network, and the Association for Quality Improvement and Productivity. He holds a Bachelor of Science degree from the University of Texas School of Communications.

A native of St. Louis, Missouri, Rich spent 30 years in Houston, Texas, before moving to Portland, Oregon, in 1996, where he and his wife have raised a son, adopted multiple Labrador retrievers, and roast and blended their own coffee. For several decades, he also has maintained a respected professional music career as a singer, harmonica player, and Americana songwriter. *Rich Layton & Tough Town* have released two critically acclaimed albums of original Texas roots rock and perform regularly at festivals and clubs throughout the Northwest. Each year, Rich makes guest appearances with Lyle Lovett, Lucinda Williams, and other long-time friends when their tours hit Portland.

Learn more at Transformcom.com and RichLayton.us
Contact Rich at rlayton@transformcom.com

Index

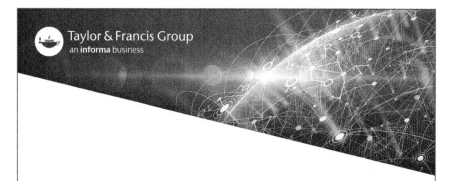

Printed in the United States
by Baker & Taylor Publisher Services